SELF-PUBLISHING: THE SECRET GUIDE TO BECOMING A BEST SELLER

RICHARD MCCARTNEY

Author Endorsement:

"As a result of your promotion, I managed to enter the Top 1000 Paid in the whole Amazon Kindle store with my debut novel, Isolated. Thank you for turning my book into a Best Seller. Overall a fantastic service."
Matt Rogers, action-thriller author of Jason King series

"Amazing result! The prestige of becoming a Best Seller is something I hoped for but thought may be out of my reach. Your support and advice on what to do proved priceless. There is clearly a lot of expertise needed to become a Best Seller without breaking the bank. I look forward to many more promotions in the future. You are the best!"
Author – Fran Connor

"You went above and beyond my expectations to help me achieve a Best Seller ranking for my book. As a first time author, it is extremely difficult to fan the flames of interest of new readers and then turn those readers into helpful, insightful reviewers, but it was achieved - the results were spectacular! My book actually received top ranking in three separate categories. I'm a believer!"
Author – Jessika Kilde

Self-Publishing:
The Secret Guide To Becoming A Best Seller

By Richard McCartney

Version 3.2

Author's note: Version 3.2 of this book includes:

- changes Amazon introduced in early 2019
- an updated Chapter 14 listing the Best Book Promotion Sites of 2019
- update of weblinks including kbookpromotions

CONTENTS

CHAPTER 1

WHY YOU NEED TO READ THIS BOOK

THE PAIN: Marketing a book is difficult for most authors. It takes an incredible lot of time, and often for no measurable results in sales. Some of you may have spent hours, days, weeks, even months, writing blogs, and getting active on Facebook and Twitter in order to promote your book. You may even have participated in author forums, or offered your book for free as part of a book promotion. Then you look at your sales figures for the last weeks or months, and your heart sinks. Why isn't this working?

The gain: I was in exactly in the same situation, in my case trying to promote my father's books, which previously enjoyed a decent amount of success in paperback format, and printed by a major publisher. The book promotions were going nowhere. Then, over time, I developed a book marketing strategy. More importantly, I established a strong and reliable group of readers, many of whom were fellow authors, to help me ensure I got as much visibility as possible, and from this, increased sales. I found a way to provide RELIABLE results. For example, I found a secure way to get a book on the Amazon Best Seller's list, a reliable way to find reviewers, and a way to get guaranteed sales!

Then I thought, 'Boy, I might not be a great writer myself, but do I know how to promote books!' Much of this was learnt from my 20+ years in marketing software and online businesses, so I asked myself, why not offer this to other authors? And so I did, and eventually created kbookpromotions.com (formerly kindlebookpromotions), an online service that has now served well over a hundred authors, guaranteeing them a Best Seller spot on Amazon, THE place to be in promoting and selling your book.

As word got out of my service, I found more and more authors wanting the "guarantee or your money back" service. I knew I was onto a winner when I saw the same authors coming back for more help, asking for ideas on how to further promote their books, and to help them launch their next book. Today, I even help established authors with their promotions, but my heart remains in helping promote the indie author who does not have the marketing prowess of the large publishers.

This book is therefore for all authors, whether in fiction or non-fiction, who are either overawed by the complexities of modern-day book marketing, or who have tried just about everything else to promote their book but met no success, and want to rely on people who provide guaranteed results in selling and promoting their books. Equally, it is for authors who want to just focus on their writing, and to outsource a good part of the marketing efforts to others with experience in doing so.

I want to start by telling you what I think are the three main mistakes authors make in trying to promote and sell their books. These are:

ONE: The belief that your book will sell by itself. You are convinced your book has great merit and nothing really has to be done but to just publish it on KDP (Kindle Direct Publishing). Wrong! You probably read about Amazon's first million-dollar authors, like John Locke, who sold one million eBooks in just 5 months. If he can do it, why can't I? Well, if you haven't heard yet, it just isn't that easy and Locke used a number of the techniques I'll be covering in this book, from promoting his book on popular book marketing services to paying for book reviews. Yes, you heard right. Even the most successful authors use whatever it takes to sell their books, and as I will uncover in this book, many of these more maverick methods for promoting your book are actually quite wide-spread. It's just that many of the more successful authors don't like to talk about it.

Even if you are convinced you have a great book (and you may be right!), don't let these fantasy success stories go to your head. Much of their success is down to hard work in marketing their book or a lot of luck, and probably even more likely, a mixture of the two. Unless you have a marketing plan in place, you are not going to make it as a commercially successful author.

TWO: The belief that social media alone will help you reach hundreds, if not thousands, of new readers. As you will discover during the course of this book, while social media can be helpful, it is unlikely to get you decent sales results. And when it comes to guaranteed results, social media is, in most cases, simply too risky. This is particularly true of services, free or paid, that promise to send out your book to tens of thousands of Facebook friends or Twitter followers. In these cases, you have to ask, why is this service free? Could it be they just want to get my email address so they can spam me? Or ask yourself, why should a certain group of Facebook users, who have never heard of me before, buy my book? Ever heard the joke, why does Voldemort use Twitter and not Facebook? The answer: Voldemort uses Twitter because he has followers, not friends. Well, social media works pretty much that way in general: you have to make friends before they'll decide to buy your book.

And let's be honest about web marketing techniques like these that try to impress you with large numbers. Whether they have thousands of Facebook friends or a million Twitter followers, or can send out an email to 1 trillion people (OK, yes, I exaggerate here, but you get my drift), the reality is that very few of them will read or even look at these promotions, much less take action on them. My hat goes off to sites like The Kindle Books and Tips blog, which at least warns you of this fact. You'll find more on this later in the book.

THREE: The belief that you can promote your book successfully for free, and not need to spend a single dollar in marketing. Wrong! Whether it's paying for a good book cover, a good professional review, or promoting your book on popular book reader sites like Goodreads, the reality is that, like professional publishers, a marketing budget has to be put aside for the promotion of your book. If you are OK with spending money on getting your book formatted or edited or proof-read, then be OK with also putting money aside for promoting your book. After all, what's the point in spending all that effort and money in writing and editing a book, if there is nobody there to find it and read it? So, get busy, and figure out ways to find new readers. The good news is that this book shows you how to do this.

"But what about all the free promotional services out there?" I hear you cry, "aren't they good enough?" The answer is no. Most of these services depend on you offering your book for free, so this means zero revenue for you. Sure, if you have 3 or 4 books already published, some of these readers might buy your other books, but don't bet on it. Ask yourself, "Why did they select my book in the first place?" That's right, because it was for free! This means that unless you offer your other books for free, they are unlikely to read your other books.

And, again, let's get real, when we say "read", what we really mean is that many of these will skim the first pages of your book, then probably abandon it. This is one of the reasons why Amazon has started counting the number of pages read in a book. They want to discourage such behavior. Now ask yourself why you get those terrible 1-star reviews for your book following a free promotion? You probably guessed it: because it's these morons (sorry, but I do dislike these trolls who trash books they haven't even read on Amazon) are expecting something better (in their esteemed eyes), even if the book was given to them for free. Grrrrr! OK, I'll calm down now, but don't these inane reviews annoy you too?

In summary, be aware of these three errors I have listed. Focus instead on marketing techniques and services that provide reliable sales results for your book. Marketing your book is about getting your book in front of the right readers, and, if possible, readers who will engage with your book and help you endorse it. These are your potential long-term followers. People who will commit to not only buying your book, but also to promoting it by writing reviews on their blogs, on Amazon, and on other sites like Goodreads.

How do you find these book promoters who can give you reliable results? How do you find these engaged readers who will promote your book? Well, read on to find out. In this book I will unveil how I found these book promoters and the methods they use to promote your books. Was it easy to find all this out? No, it was darn hard. Much of my discovery came out of several years of trying to do this for the authors who hired my help to achieve this.

I learnt a lot of powerful and, in many cases, undisclosed secrets within Amazon along the way, but the bedrock of finding a way to provide reliable results lies in building up a network of trusted book lovers over a good number of years. I wish I could show you a step-by-step process by which you could build a similar network yourself, but if it was that easy, then anyone could do it. And as you have already probably worked out from your own experiences, eBook marketing is hard, and very few people provide guaranteed sales results.

So, read on to discover how this is done.

NOTE: This book assumes you have basic knowledge of publishing your book on KDP (Kindle Direct Publishing) and of Amazon's basic promotional services, such as Kindle Countdown and Kindle's Free Promotion service. If I refer to anything related to Amazon you are not familiar with, you can quite easily look it up on the Internet.

CHAPTER 2

YOUR GIFT

THANK you for purchasing this book. As a bonus, you can request a free copy of my other book The *Unofficial Authors' Guide To Buying And Selling Your Book On Amazon: The Top 5 Cheat Sheet*. It has over 100 reviews and reached #1 in the Amazon Best Seller lists in its genre.

Reviews posted about this book on Amazon:

"A Wonderful Resource for Aspiring Authors"
"Fabulous Tips for Anyone Publishing on Amazon"
"A Must Read for Indie Authors"
"I cannot recommend this book strongly enough"
"A crucial book for anyone choosing to self publish"

This book is normally priced between $0.99 and $7.99, and provides some very useful tips about selling books on Amazon. For your free copy, simply send me an email request at the following address:

richard@kbookpromotions.com

Yes, feel free to email me now before you get totally absorbed into the rest of this book.

NOTE: and if you get to reach the end of this book, an even bigger present awaits you - hold on and see!

CHAPTER 3

INTRODUCTION: THE BREAKTHROUGH

YOU WILL HAVE HEARD this before, but to be sure, let me shout it out loud and clear: The best place to promote your book and make sales is on Amazon. It remains the number one site for book sales, hands down. So, if you are really looking for the most effective way to market your book, it's not by what happens outside the Amazon.com website, but what happens within it. Capiche? Comprende? I don't know how loud I have to say this to help you focus primarily on Amazon, but please believe me when I tell you that my breakthrough moment was when I stopped all promotion efforts on social media and other sites, and concentrated on just Amazon.com.

Yes, there are other sites where you can sell your books, like Barnes & Noble and the Apple Store, but none come near the sales numbers of Amazon. Amazon remains THE place to promote and sell your books, especially eBooks.

Just as the major food suppliers fight it out to get the prime spot in a supermarket, knowing they bring the best sales results, authors have to figure out the best places to display their books in the biggest and most important book supermarket of them all – Amazon. Do you want to have your book stuck behind three stacks of tinned peas somewhere on the 7th shelf, or in the front row counter of a corner aisle where the supermarket gets the most visitors? Added to this, authors have to figure out how Amazon decides which books to promote above others. Ever been to supermarkets where you have heard announcements on the loud speakers encouraging you to try out product X at "today's special discount price"? That's right, it happens nearly all the time, and Amazon has its own way of shouting out loud about certain books it wants to promote.

If you can make your book visible on Amazon and help ensure Amazon selects your book for promotion, then you are on the right track to success, catching the eyes of hundreds, if not thousands, of potential Amazon book buyers.

OK, now I've touched on the best way to promote your book, let's really get started. Let's learn more about how this is actually done.

CHAPTER 4

"THE GOOD, THE BAD, AND THE UGLY": THE WRONG WAY TO PROMOTE YOUR BOOK

NOTE: This chapter is full of stats. For those who find stats boring, you might want to skip some of the following pages, but this chapter does contain useful advice on what works and does not work when trying to promote your book, so bear with me.

DO you want to hear the good news or the bad news first?

Let's be different. We'll start with the ugly news. Many authors will find the following more than a little discouraging, but ultimately it will point us in the right direction – the right way to promote your book.

THE UGLY:

This might surprise you, but the ugly way to promote your book is by using social media. Heed my words: beware of using social media, or better said, beware of investing a lot of time on social media. Sports stars use it, politicians use it, journalists use it, kids use it, hey, even the neighbor's dog probably uses social media. Everyone uses it! So, who am I to warn you about using social media? Don't get me wrong. Facebook and Twitter might be great for sharing news and pictures and for getting updates from others on what is going on. But it's also great for getting lots of trashy information, such as what a certain celebrity ate for dinner. While social media does have some value, it is rarely of any use at all for converting social media visitors to buyers of your book. And that's what you really want, right? To find new readers for your book.

Let me now introduce you to some terms you might be unfamiliar with from the world of online marketing. Let's start with CTR (click-through rates), a term made popular by Google to explain how to measure the success of Google AdWords – that's those sponsored links you often find at the top of Google search results.

I come from a background in online marketing, and any online marketer worth her or his salt will know of Google AdWords, email software, or marketing automation tools. They will also know of the following stats I'm about to share with you when it comes to click-through rates.

Let's first clarify what a click-through rate is. This is the percentage of people that click on a link or advertising banner for your book. You also need to know about conversion rates. Conversion rates (or "conversions" for short) are the percentage of people who clicked on your link and then went on to buy your book. So, what's this got to do with social media? Bear with me.

To sell a book through social media sites such as Facebook or Twitter, or even your own blog page, you have to have a link or banner image to your book page on Amazon, and from here the visitor has to then click the "buy" button.

OK, brace yourself because here comes the really ugly news – which is a real shocker. The shocking (but true) stats about banner images are their very poor click-through rates. The average CTR is just 0.05% (according to latest figures from SmartInsights). So that's just 5 clicks per 1000 visitors!

Did I make a typo mistake here? No, you heard right the first time.

The click-through rate is just 0.05%!
So just 5 clicks per 1000 visitors

Boy, does that look ugly! In fact, it's abysmal.

What's that? You don't believe these stats? Then check it out yourself on Google. The source I gave is as good as it gets, but for further confirmation you can search on Google or Bing for ""0.05% average CTR", you should find similar results from other respected sources, such as Acquisio or HubSpot.

Agreed – these are ugly figures – but what if I were to improve the odds by using the real powerhouses of the social media world? What if I was to advertise on Facebook and Twitter that get millions of visitors each day? What if I pay for a banner promoting my book on these sites – surely the results would be better then?

Well, let's look at the stats based on the latest SmartInsights benchmark results. Again, look this up on Google if you don't believe me. According to SmartInsights, you can expect the following results:

Facebook: an average CTR of 0.0119%

Twitter: an average CTR of 1%

Now, this really breaks my heart. This means that when using the real power houses of social media such as Facebook just 11 from 1000 people will click on my book display ad on. Twitter would generate better results, but still depressingly low.

Now, brace yourself once more, as we move on to the bad news.

CHAPTER 5

THE BAD - THE WRONG WAY TO PROMOTE YOUR BOOK

THE BAD:

If you thought the click-through rates for social media banners were depressing, get ready for even worse news, as we look at the equally shocking (but equally true) stats for conversion rates.

Let's remind ourselves, we have two main steps to convert your visitors into buyers of your book:

Step 1: Getting them to click on your banner or link (click-through rates).

Step 2: Getting them to buy your book on Amazon (conversion rates).

If we are to believe the benchmark results from independent sources, then the omens are not great – in fact, they are shockingly bad.

According to GoldSpot Media, 50% of clicks on mobile ads (which could be banner ads they found on your blog page or an ad you paid for on Facebook or Twitter) are accidental. According to BannerSnack, 54% of users don't even click on banner ads because they don't trust them. And according to UnBounce, 99% of advertisers are wasting money on ads.

Can you believe these percentages? Don't they just make you want to shrivel up and die? But don't give up yet. There is light at the end of the tunnel, but it is time we woke up to the realities of using social media. Just like rabbits that stand frozen in front of oncoming car headlights, we need to snap out of it. It's time to wake up and smell the coffee, and move on, because social media isn't the way forward in getting you good book sales. Still dazzled by those attractive lights of social media? Still not believing what I am saying?

Let's get right down to looking at the conversion rate numbers, and see if your logical mind snaps you out of it.

Imagine you have successfully gotten your first visitor to click on your banner or link on your blog page that takes her or him to your Amazon book page. In theory, they are now just one click away from buying your book. So, what are the chances of them buying the book by clicking on the "buy" button?

Well, let's look at the stats. For this, we will turn to the giants of online advertising, Google and Amazon. According to Sherpa, a very credible research firm specializing in tracking what works in all aspects of marketing, for Google Ads you can expect a conversion rate of about 1 to 5 percent. They state that a quarter of all advertisers get less than 1% conversion rates, while the top 25 percent get a conversion rate of 5%. Since few authors are online experts, you could expect conversion rates of 1%.

Let's be optimistic and say authors could get conversion rates of 3%.

Now let's look at how Amazon adverts work. Not all authors are even aware that you can run advertising banners on Amazon, although it's been available for quite some time now. If you run a search on Google for "average conversion rates for Amazon Ads", you should come across an Amazon forum I found where advertisers state that the average conversion rate for their Amazon Ads is 3%. Good, we have an agreed-upon average conversion rate of 3% on both Google and Amazon.

Stay with me here because I know stats can put some readers to sleep or cause them to just switch off. This is worth paying attention to, so stay focused on the next details I am about to share with you.

If 3% is the average conversion rate on Amazon, then this means that only 3 of each 100 people clicking on your banner ad or link on your blog page will go on to press that "buy" button on Amazon and purchase your book. This is bad, really bad - especially if we put together the whole picture. Let's do the math.

Assuming we have a blog site with 1000 unique visitors a month (yes, I know, if only our blog sites attracted such numbers!), and there is a banner ad there encouraging all visitors to buy your book on Amazon. This is how the math would play out:

1000 visitors x 0.005% click-thru rate = 5 clicks.
5 x 3% conversion rate = 0.15.
So not even 1 book sale a month!

Take a moment to absorb this.

Sheesh! Now I'm really depressed. So, if I was actively blogging for a whole year, and I got 1000 visitors per month, I would not even get one quarter of sale per month, and nearly 2 sales a year (0.15 x 12 = 1.8 sales).

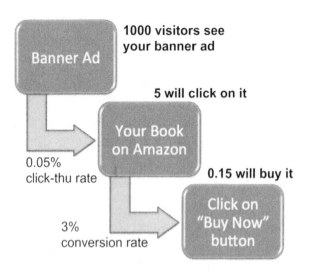

Typical conversion rates

Wow, why didn't someone show me this before?! And we have been optimistic with our numbers here. In most cases, authors will get far fewer visitors a month (probably in the hundreds at best) and a lower conversion rate of probably 1%.

What?! This cannot be! Can it?

Well, if you pop in your own average visitor numbers for your web site, Facebook page, or blog site, and use the average CTR and conversion rates shown above, you'll be able to calculate the results yourself. Better yet, don't go there. You won't want to see the numbers.

Someone pass me the box of tissues, because even grown men should weep looking at these numbers. Better yet, pass me the morphine!

Hang on a minute! These numbers can't be right. They just can't be. OK, let's assume our blog page is already visited by a loyal fan base and the pages you publish are the best thing since sliced bread and you have a much higher conversion rate. How much better than the average could it be? Twice as good? Three times as good? Even 10 times as good?

OK, let's kid ourselves and say that our results would be 10 times better than the average, then our sales would be 1.5 sales per month. That's still incredibly dismal.

Well, we are hardly going to break out the champagne and book ourselves the next available cruise to the Caribbean on these numbers. So, let's not give up our day jobs just yet.

I could explain why your sales results through social media would probably be even worse than the estimates I have given (for example, how many of the people clicking through to your Amazon page even have a Kindle to purchase your eBook?), but I think I've proven my point already.

And before I get an avalanche of hate emails from social media fans shouting me down for even doubting the value of social media, let me say that social media can have a value. It's just not in the lead when it comes to sales generation for authors who want to sell books. I've found social media to be great for opening doors to other people I did not know before, as well as for sharing opinions and having discussions. All good and well, but NOT for helping sell eBooks.

Social media fans may want to set their dogs, cats, even guinea pigs on me, but it isn't going to change these real stats I have shared with you.

It's time to try something besides social media, and this is where the good news starts. After all, now I've given you the bad news, it's only fair that I give you the good news.

CHAPTER 6

THE GOOD - THE RIGHT WAY TO PROMOTE YOUR BOOK

The Good – Book Promotion Services

IT SHOULD COME as no surprise that there are "good" ways to promote your book – ones that help you find new readers and new sales, and some of these even provide guaranteed results. Of these, the ones I would recommend the most are book subscription services, sometimes also called "email subscription services". These service providers spotted a huge gap in the market when Amazon introduced eBooks and Kindle Direct Publishing (KDP), allowing practically anyone to make their books available as Kindle Books on Amazon. With so many new eBooks hitting the market, they realized that what most readers really want are decent books at bargain prices. Just as when you walk into a bookstore and are offered "2 for 3" book offers, or this month's special discount offers, the new generation of eBook readers want the same thing.

Yet Amazon and many publishers started raising the price of eBooks instead, using the usual sales strategy of raising prices for things that are in demand and selling well. And, boy, did eBooks really take off! They have proven popular not only to readers who can find and download the next book they want to read instantly, but publishers and booksellers who adored the profit margins they could make from them. With eBooks, there are no print costs, no distribution costs, no postage costs... Practically no costs at all once the book is available on any online retail store such as Amazon. With demand for eBooks outstripping demand for printed books, neither Amazon nor any publisher wanted to lower their book prices, so they offered few real marketing opportunities to promote books at a discount price. But the book subscription services did.

They wrote to authors and stated that if they offered their book for a discount price on an agreed promotion date, they would send emails out to potential book buyers informing them that your book was available at a bargain price. And the best bargain of all was if your book was offered for free, so the free book offer became immensely popular. All authors had to do was to pay a certain fee for advertising their book in the service's email, and the book would be seen by thousands (now millions) of eBook readers looking for bargain or free books. And, bang, the eBook subscription service was born, and, oh man, how it took off!

In a matter of months, book subscription services like BookBub, BookGorilla, eReader News Today, kbookpromotions(which I have been involved in from its early beginnings), and many others took off. Of these, probably BookBub is the best known and most successful. So successful did it become, that in 2014 it announced it had received over $3.8 million in funding from investors such as Next-View Ventures, Avalon Ventures, and Bloomberg Beta, who were clearly convinced of their potential to make money. And you don't have to be a genius to work out why. For reasons we have already explored, authors have no other reliable ways to promote their books.

Today, BookBub can ask authors to pay anything from $470 to $2350 for books in the genre Crime Fiction, although pricing does vary a little by genre. For this, an author can expect thousands of downloads of their book if offered for free, and several hundred in sales if your book is offered at a discount price of $0.99 or over. What is even better, if you are an author with several books published on Kindle, there is the additional benefit that some of these buyers might go on to purchase your other books.

Some authors might find paying sums of up to $2350 rather expensive, if not exorbitant, to have your book promoted in a BookBub email that is sent to thousands of potential book buyers. A very large number of authors, however, seem to be very happy to pay this price to promote their book. After all, there is a certain feeling of exuberance when seeing your book downloaded by thousands of readers, or your book sold in the several hundreds in a day or two. This comes with the added bonus that your book is very likely to be in the Amazon Best Seller lists. Indeed, BookBub is in the luxurious position of turning down most authors who apply for their services. It is well known that they have long waiting lists of applicants willing to pay for their services.

Are authors wrong to spend this kind of money in advertising their books? Well, let's do the math. If we were to carry out an ROI (return on investment) examination comparing book subscription services to social media, what would we see?

We learned earlier that through social media, 1000 visitors through your blog site would generate no better than one sale a month. Now compare this to 1 email sent out by book subscription services like BookBub generating an average of 3,930 copies sold. This is the average sales number BookBub gives on their website (at time of writing this book).

Wow. That's quite a difference. It really is no competition.

Book subscription services win hands down. Game. Set. And Match.

Admittedly, you have to pay substantial money to use book subscription services, but the advantages are very clear. If you were to continue to just use social media, it could take you more than your lifetime to achieve sales of 3,930 books.

What makes it even more remarkable is that book subscription services deliver these kinds of sales results not in a month, but in just about 3 to 5 days!

Just think of the time saved in hours, days, weeks, months if you concentrated on book subscription services rather than writing continuously on blogs, Facebook, and Twitter. Assume one blog article takes you one hour to write and publish (and believe me, it usually takes longer than just the hour), and one blog generates 1000 visitors in a month, which converts to (let's be optimistic and say) 1 in sales. That means that to get 3,930 books sold, you would have had to spend close to 3,930 hours.

By Grabthar's Hammer! That's frightening!

That's about 23 weeks, or near 6 months of your time.

So it would take you as good as half a year of your precious time to achieve something a book subscription service ad could achieve in just 3 to 5 days.

I rest my case.

For the reasons I have just given, BookBub has become very successful, perhaps too successful. Today, it's very difficult to have our books accepted by BookBub. There are some well-informed authors who go as far as to say that BookBub has abandoned indie authors in favor of the big publishing companies who want a piece of this sales action, and are prepared to pay big bucks for it. BookBub revealed as much when they advertised for new account managers, mentioning they would focus on large publishers.

Authors applying to have their books promoted on BookBub can expect their applications to be rejected. BookBub is well known to have a very high rejection rate. What's even more annoying to authors is that they rarely explain why they have rejected a book. Don't get me wrong, BookBub is great, but your chance of getting selected is very small.

BookBub can effectively cherry-pick, selecting the books they find the most attractive. Like most book subscription services, they position themselves to offer the best books at bargain prices to their readers. But we should not forget that these subscription services do not make money from the readers, but from the authors and publishers who pay big bucks to get advertised.

So do consider using BookBub, but it's also important to look at alternative book promoters. I'll mention the best book promotion sites (or book subscription services) later on in this book, since I'm sure you are now asking, "Who are they? When can I start using them?"

The good news is that there are a good handful of them, so while you are unlikely to be accepted by BookBub, there are others you can definitely try. I certainly encourage you to try them out, even if some of them are rather expensive. After all, do you really want to try the alternative route of focusing on social media given the conversion figures I have shared?

The real question I get from many authors these days is, "If book subscription services are the way to go in getting lots of downloads and sales for my book, which of them deliver the best value for money? They all cost money, so which ones should I spend my money on?" To try and answer this question, I would like to introduce you to the eBook Marketing Magic Quadrant.

CHAPTER 7

HOW TO FIND THE BEST BOOK PROMOTERS : USING THE EBOOK MARKETING MAGIC QUADRANT

ONE OF THE hardest questions to answer from the many authors who correspond with me is, "What is the best way to promote my book?" Here's an example of the type of email request I get:

"Richard – thanks for offering your help. I've had poor sales up to now, and just can't seem to get my book off the ground. I've tried a number of ways to promote my book but with little effect. What can I do to make my book more visible and improve sales?"

I can understand their frustration. They have spent weeks, if not months, writing their book. The have paid to get it edited and proof-read and even formatted for eBook readers like Amazon's Kindle. Then, when they launch their book, nothing really seems to happen. Some small sales numbers trickle in, but then nothing. No sales, no reviews.

The reality is that to promote your book, you are going to need a budget and a certain amount of your time. If money has to be put aside to market your book, the question is, "How can I get the best value for my money in promoting my book?" Without a budget, you are frankly going to be totally lost or incredibly lucky in successfully selling your book. And if you are going to depend on luck, well, prepare to be disappointed.

Over the years I have spent promoting many authors' books, I have found two main groups of authors in terms of marketing strategy. Those that go for "everything for free where possible", and those that understand that money does have to be spent to promote their books. Guess which type of author ends up being the most successful? The difficulty lies in figuring out the best way to spend our marketing dollars as authors. I have come across many different methods, techniques, and players all claiming to deliver incredible results. There are some sharks out there, but there are also some really good guys who deliver on what they promise. To help authors out, I devised the eBook Marketing Magic Quadrant.

There are so many discussions out there about how to sell your book that it's difficult to make out the good from the bad, to work out which are the best practices you should follow, and the pitfalls you should avoid. There is no one way to promote your book, so you need to try out many of the different alternatives and see which ones work for you, and which ones do not. This can take a lot of time, and a decent amount of money. The good news is that I have tried many of these already for many of the authors I have worked with. For this reason, I seriously recommend you use this Magic Quadrant before launching any new book so you can figure out the best ways to spend your own money.

The Magic Quadrant addresses two main questions that need to be considered in determining the best way to spend your marketing money. These are:

1. Which will deliver the Best Revenue?
2. Which have the Best Reach?

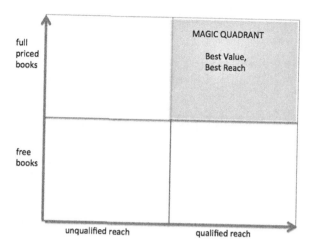

The Magic Quadrant

Looking at the Magic Quadrant diagram I have provided, the best option for authors is to find anything that fits in the top right quadrant, as this delivers both the best revenue and the best engagement. Let's now look at each of the axes of the Magic Quadrant.

Best revenue: which will provide the most money in sales?

We'll cover this in more detail later in the book when we explore the best ways to increase revenues earned from your book, but for the purposes of how it fits into the Magic Quadrant, the following quick summary should suffice.

The main way to make revenue from your book is through royalties.

So, promotions that:

1. Offer your books for free generate no immediate revenue.

2. Offer your book at a discount price of just $0.99 earn you 35% royalty
3. Offer your book at $2.99 or more deliver the best revenue, with royalties of 70% (on Amazon KDP)

Free book promotions:

Free book promotions have become very popular, but much of this is due to the mistaken belief that they can generate good sales results for the author. Before, this could have been the case because Amazon's Best Seller lists did not distinguish free books from priced books.

So, if you offered your book for free for 3 days, it could reach very high in the Amazon Sales Ranking and so turn your book into an Amazon Best Seller. When your book no longer became free, it would still appear in the Paid Best Seller lists for a while. So, if your book price changed from $0 to $2.99, it could earn you a good number of sales since it was very visible in the top Amazon Best Seller lists.

No more. Amazon discovered this loophole and separated the Best Seller lists into Free and Paid Best Seller lists. Once your book is no longer free, it moves quickly to the Paid lists with a far lower Amazon Sales Ranking and very likely outside the Best Seller lists.

The result of this change is that authors make no revenue at all from free book promotions. If you get a thousand downloads of your book during a free book promotion, you will make zero dollars. The main advantage of the free promotion is that it makes your book far more visible through the many free book promotion sites that offer your book. So, hopefully, a good number of readers who download your free book will like it enough to want to buy another book from you, especially if the book is part of a series. But don't hold your breath on this one. In general, people who want free books only (or mostly) select other free books.

WARNING: In 2017, David Gaughran's blog site alerted many readers and Amazon of the fraudulent practice of click farming. This is the practice of using machines (or computer programs) to download thousands of free books. So, be careful of promoters promising over 10,000 downloads of your free book. If their offer looks too good to be true, then it probably is. It's not people downloading your free book, but machines.

NOTE: It seems that these click-farms only target free books since they clearly don't want to risk using their credit cards to download thousands of paid or discounted book. So going for discounted book promotions seems to be the safe bet going forward.

Discount book promotions:

These have become more popular as more and more authors have begun to realize that free book promotions are not for them. This could be because authors don't like to offer one of their books (permanently) for free, or they have come to realize that there is no, or little, money to be earned from it. The download number for discount book offers is far smaller than for free book promotions, but at least you do earn 35% royalties from each book sold. So, for example, if you get 100 sales of your book at $0.99, you make $35 (100x$0.99x0.35= $35).

$2.99 plus promotions:

These promotions are much harder to find, but they clearly deliver the best revenue for the author since you are earning 70% on them. So, let's compare the situation if you sell 100 books with 70% royalty:

100 sales x $2.99 book price x 0.70 royalty = $209

Wow. That's a big difference from the $35 you earn for discounted books with a royalty of just 35%.

The difference is so big that even if you sell just half the amount compared to a discount book offer, you end up making more money.

Here are the sums for you:

50 sales x $2.99 book price x 0.70 royalty = $105

That's still three times more revenue than if you ran a discount book promotion.

Clearly, the promotional services that offer your book at $2.99 or over bring the best revenue opportunities. The challenge is in finding those that can deliver a decent volume in sales.

These days, I see a lot of books priced at $2.99 or $3.99, and that makes a lot of sense to me. $2.99 is the minimum price you can offer for a book earning 70% royalty, so this balances offering the cheapest price to the reader (so they are not put off by a high price), and still earning 70% royalty for the author.

Best reach:

This next criteria point is all about the promotional services that get you the best response from the readers. This can be measured by the quality of the people they can reach and how the readers they attract will engage with your book. There are three main types here, starting with those considered to have an "unqualified reach", those with a "qualified reach", and best of all, those with "best engagement". Let's explain each of these groups in more detail.

Unqualified reach:

"Reach" is about how many people your book is reaching. For online marketers, this is often called "impressions", a term coined and made popular by Google for those wishing to measure the effectiveness of Google AdWords – these are the little ads you usually find on the first page of Google when you enter a search word. Impressions are the number of times your ad will have been "displayed" in front of other users. Please note that "displayed" does not necessarily mean the user actually noticed it – just that the ad appeared on their screens. In a similar way, you will get book promotion touts boasting about how many people they have on the email distribution list (thousands, maybe even millions).

So, when they send out an email with your book cover on it, it could be displayed to thousands of users. Equally, if your book is one of many in the email list, and appearing "below the fold" (so users have to scroll down their email to see it), then most of the audience will not even see your book cover, let alone notice it.

The same is true of promoters telling you about the huge number of Facebook friends they have, or the massive list of Twitter followers they have, and who can be informed about your book. These types of promotions are nearly worthless since the audience they reach is not filtered or qualified in any way. For example, if I have 10,000 Twitter followers (something I can get quite quickly with some Fiverr gigs), and I mention your book to them, does that mean any of them are likely to buy your book? I don't think so. This is what some might call cold, cold, cold (if not freezing) calling. None of these people know you, or even stated they like to read books.

As you will discover, it is not always easy to distinguish the good guys from the bad guys in this sector of the market. The best advice I can give you is to run a quick search for them on Google. Do they even have a website? If Company X claims they can really help you and have helped hundreds of other authors, see if they have a website. If their email address is johndoe@CompanyX.com, then check if the website www.CompanyX.com or www.CompanyX.net exists. If not, then I would discourage you from using them.

Also, beware of $5 to $20 Twitter or Facebook packages promising to reach tens of thousands of followers or friends. Most of these followers are often gamed, gained through $5 Fiverr gigs or other inappropriate means. The general advice is to stay away from these types of providers. $5 might not sound like much, but if it delivers zero results, then it is a waste. Admittedly, you can find some good gigs on Fiverr, but not in this area. In all fairness to the people offering you these types of gigs, they are often delivering on what they promise. They will send a promotional link of your book to their many followers, but few, if any, of these followers will actually go ahead and click on the link. So, it's not about the volume of people you can reach, but the quality of the people you can reach.

Qualified reach:

These are the vendors who make some clear effort to qualify the audiences they promote to authors. This could be by providing a list of Goodreads subscribers (who are very likely to be book readers), or a list that has been filtered by age, gender, or (even better) by their preferred book genres. This is where vendors such as BookBub excel, by promoting your book to email subscribers whose preferred book genre matches the genre of your book. So, if BookBub has 10,530 subscribers in the genre "Science Fiction", and this matches your genre, then you know how many people your book could potentially reach, and because they all like Science Fiction, there is a decent chance they will be interested in your book.

Another good example would be vendors like Book Marketing Tools. They have an online application which, for just $29, will submit your book to multiple free promotions sites, saving you considerable time. It has a wizard that takes you about 15 minutes to complete, and at the end of it, submits your book to 20+ sites on an agreed promotion date. In this case, their target audience is people who like to receive free books. Using the Magic Quadrant, this vendor would score quite highly in their "reach", but not score so highly in delivering the "best revenue", since authors make no direct money from their books being offered for free.

Another vendor I like in this group is Books Butterfly. Not only do they provide free book promotions, but also discount book promotions at $0.99 – so authors can earn some royalties here. What I particularly like about them is that they provide guaranteed results or a refund. This is very important, since authors at least know what sort of result they can expect if they invest their money in such promotional vendors.

Kindle Daily Nation is another that I also like. Not only do they provide an eBook Tracker that monitors your Amazon Sales Rank, but they also publish expected results. They do not guarantee results, but providing expected results based on the results of their customers is also great to see.

Best engagement:

These vendors are much harder to find, but deserve your attention. They do not only find buyers for your book, but readers that will actively engage with your book by promoting it in their blogs, providing likes for it on social media, or writing reviews of your book on influential sites like Goodreads, Amazon, or Barnes and Noble. BookBub is on the borderline between a vendor that provides "qualified reach" and "best engagement". They are clearly strong in matching your book to readers who match your genre, so while BookBub makes no commitment to getting these readers to engage with your book further than reading it, there is a chance that some of them will, by writing reviews on Amazon or Goodreads.

A vendor that clearly fits into the "best engagement" group is Goodreads. They actively invite all their members to list the books they have read and plan to read, and to write reviews about each book. Let's face it, any reader that spends her or his own time writing a review of your book is of great value to you. They are, in effect, advertising your book on the Internet.

The other vendor I would place in this group is kbookpromotions.com, the company I founded. I simply saw a gap in the market. I could not find any vendor that could promote books at $2.99 or over (enabling authors to receive 70% royalties); provide engaged readers who have a profile of writing book reviews on their blogs, Goodreads, or Amazon; and provide guaranteed results.

Why best engagement has the highest value:

It should come as no surprise that engagement has the highest value. Finding a reader that comments, likes, shares, reviews, or recommends your book is of tremendous value. They are like gold! They can potentially become a fan, reading several, if not all, of your books. They are showing a level of loyalty and commitment not found in any of the other quadrants in the Magic Quadrant graph. They can become social media evangelists, blog champions, and beta readers of your book. They are the type of readers who may well purchase your book before it is even available, as a Pre-Order on Amazon.

Developing your own list of engaged readers takes a great deal of time, effort, money (through the promotions you run to find them), and marketing knowhow. It's all about establishing and maintaining a relationship with people that like your type of books and will recommend them to others. For this reason, you should choose promotions in this engagement quadrant as much as possible. Look for promotional packages that provide guaranteed results, if possible. By all means, also consider promotions in the other quadrants that are often cheaper in price. But those in the unqualified reach category should never be your primary channel for selling and promoting your books, but part of a larger launch plan.

The difficulty for most authors is finding the time or even having the inclination to find engaged readers. It can be an all-consuming business.

Here is a list of actions authors can take to engage with readers:

- Giving away copies of books with personalized thank-you notes

- Polling cover images or character names
- Hosting weekly Twitter chats
- Posting videos about a book
- Sharing chapter reveals
- Commenting on reviews left on Goodreads
- Sending email updates about upcoming novels
- Setting up forums or groups on Facebook or Google+ to encourage discussion

... Wait, wait, wait. Stop this right now.

It exhausts me just to look at this list of actions. Few authors have the time to do these things. Can't I just hire someone who can find these engaged readers for me?

Whether you are an author who just wants to write books and leave marketing to others, or an author who wants to expand your reach to new engaged readers, I invite you to take a good look at kbookpromotions.com. This service provides a shortcut, a way to save hours of time and find engaged readers, with a track record in taking actions on social media or writing reviews on Goodreads or Amazon. It also delivers guaranteed results.

OK – so far, we have gone through the wrong (the bad and the ugly) ways to market your book. We also covered the right ways to market your book, and that this requires a certain budget if you want to get effective results. And lastly, through the eBook Marketing Magic Quadrant, I have tried to guide you towards the best ways to spend your marketing money, ensuring that you invest in services that deliver the best revenue opportunity and the best engagement. Now, let's look at the actual best ways to find new readers for your book.

CHAPTER 8

THE BEST WAYS TO FIND
READERS FOR YOUR BOOK

SO, how do readers look for books? In my book introduction, I mentioned that it's all about making sure your book is found on Amazon, the only on-line bookstore that really counts. Of course, there are other places, but Amazon is the undisputed leader. I could show you stats to confirm this, but it would not take you long to figure this out for yourself if you search for this information on Google or Bing.

Another way to confirm this is to simply ask yourself when was the last time you purchased an eBook based on something you found elsewhere on the internet, such as in someone's blog. Not very recently (if ever), right? Now ask yourself, when was the last time you purchased a book you found on Amazon? Much more recently, correct?

So, how do most Amazon customers find and purchase books on Amazon? I believe the answer lies mainly in the following ways:

1. They search for an author or book title they are already interested in. This can be done as easily from their

Kindle device as from a computer, iPad, or Smartphone while browsing on the Amazon store.

2. They browse through the Top 100 Best Sellers on Amazon; usually in the book categories they like most.
3. They look at the Hot New Releases section on Amazon.
4. They see a book in the "Customers Who Bought This Item Also Bought" section.
5. They browse through the book categories they like on Amazon. If you are a reader of Historical Romance novels, you will probably buy other books from the same genre.
6. They use the autocomplete suggestion in the Amazon search box.

Now, time for a reality check. Although there are no stats I know of on this, I suspect as much as 80 to 90 percent of readers use the first method, selecting authors or books they already know or have heard of. This also falls under the "word of mouth" category, since it's only after you've been recommended a book that you will search for it on Amazon.

You might not like to hear this, but there is very little you can do in the short term to influence this very large market segment. Authors like John Green, JK Rowling, Stephanie Meyer, Jo Nesbo, Veronica Roth, James Patterson, and other established author names fit this category well. That's why they constitute less than 1 percent of the authors on Amazon making a truckload of money with the additional help of big publishers spending big bucks to promote their books.

The good news is that we can do something about the other five categories I have listed. That's 20% of the buyers that you can influence – and that 20% is absolutely massive if you consider the millions of book buyers that visit the Amazon store.

Your marketing and sales strategy should focus on how to get into each of these key areas of Amazon I have listed:

- The Top 100 Best Seller lists
- The Hot New Releases
- The "Customers Who Bought This Item Also Bought" section
- The best eBook category for your book
- The autocomplete search results

And, as we will discover, there are lesser-known areas of Amazon to also target:

- The Popularity Lists
- The Movers and Shakers

These are the areas to focus on because, if done well, Amazon will then turn its lean and mean sales machine to your advantage, displaying your book on its web pages and email newsletters.

And here I want to stop just to stress just how good Amazon is at doing this.

When Amazon recommends a book on its site, it's no mere coincidence. This giant online retail store uses a number of methods to figure out what are the best books to display for each individual visitor to its store.

That's right – each individual visitor, I said.

Through the use of cookies on your computer and other means to work out your buying preferences, it will display certain books in front of you. This could be based on what you have recently bought, items currently in your virtual shopping cart, or even books you have browsed previously. It could be items you've rated or reviewed, and even what other customers like you have viewed and purchased.

Amazon uses individual behavioral profiling on a "personalization platform" as part of their algorithm to uniquely personalize your browsing experience each time you return to their store. So, if you are a movie buff, you can expect to see books on Hollywood and popular films and actors. If you love fictional romance, you can expect to see many books of this genre displayed on your screen.

Judging from Amazon's success, their recommendation system works extremely well. Much of their growth is arguably down to the way they have integrated their recommendations into nearly every stage of the purchasing process, from product discovery to checkout. Go to Amazon.com and you'll find multiple sections with product suggestions from "Frequently Bought Together" to "Customers Who Bought This Item Also Bought".

Amazon does not stop there. It also sends out recommendations to users through email. So, if you recently purchased an X-Men comic book, you will find similar graphic novel titles in your email.

Amazon even uses A/B email testing to determine the best type of email to convert you into a one-click buyer from the emails they send. The email with the highest "click to sales" rate will ultimately be sent to you, and changed again if you do not react to the emails it is sending you. In this way, only the most effective email invitations will reach your inbox. In fact, the conversion rate and efficiency of these emails are even more effective than the onsite recommendations Amazon gives you, with a conversion rate as high as 60% in some cases.

So, what do these emails look like? Let's look at some of the typical emails I get from Amazon in my Inbox. These are the types of emails millions of other buyers also receive.

The first one we'll look at is the typical sort of email to expect based on the categories I have purchased on Amazon:

"Dear Amazon.com Customer,
Looking for romance books at low prices? Browse this
month's deals and save up to 85% on more than 1,000
Kindle books. These deals run until the end of
this month."

Interesting. So, they clearly know the books I am looking at on their store.

I even get an email recommendation each time I purchase a book. In this case, I get an "Order Confirmation" email with a link in it to other "recommended books".

It doesn't stop there. I received this email simply because I was browsing a few pages on Amazon:

"Richard,
Based on your recent visit, we thought you might be
interested in these items."

The main point in showing you all these examples is, I hope, clear. If you can get your book on the Amazon radar, it will clearly do what it can to sell your book, and there is no better salesman in the world for your book than Amazon itself.

Throughout this book I will show you what I believe are the most effective ways to get your book noticed on Amazon. If you achieve this, then you are well on your way to having a successful book on your hands.

Let's go through each of these key areas I have listed, starting with how to get your book on the Amazon Best Seller lists.

CHAPTER 9

HOW TO MAKE YOUR BOOK A BEST SELLER

IF MANY POTENTIAL buyers look through the Best Seller categories on Amazon, how can you make sure your book reaches the Amazon Top 20 Best Seller lists, or even reach #1 for that matter?

Amazon Best Sellers

Most book promotion experts will tell you that to become a Best Seller on Amazon, you need:

1. A decent book that is well written and with no editorial flaws
2. A decent cover
3. A fair number of reviews
4. As a result of this, sales.

Of these the only ones that really count in order of priority are:

- Sales
- A fair number of reviews (the more, the better)
- A decent book cover

That's it. Nothing else. Yes, I know, this might surprise a lot of people, but Amazon doesn't really care about how good your book is (after all, one person's medicine can be another person's poison, so this is always hard to judge). What matters is if it can sell. Getting reviews is also important because it can help convert a visitor into a buyer, and therefore, improve sales. Additionally, many book promotion sites will only accept your book if it has a decent star rating and a fair number of reviews, and book promotions also could affect your sales.

Amazon's algorithms add weight to the number of reviews you get, especially new ones and any helpful votes they might get. They now use this to calculate the overall star rating for your book. So, reviews are clearly seen as important in persuading potential readers to buy.

It's no coincidence that the way Amazon designs the page layout of your book is to show very prominently how many stars and reviews your book has received. So, do not underestimate the importance of reviews in the mind of Amazon, and in potentially increasing your book sales.

It's all about first impressions and how that can influence the potential buyer. Having many reviews indicates there are a lot of people reading your book. If it reaches over 100 reviews, it suggests the book has gone mainstream and has a large reader community. Similarly, having a decent book cover is influential in the first impressions it gives to the online visitor. A book with a poor-quality book cover and ugly fonts could just persuade the online shopper to look elsewhere.

Let me repeat this since it's important. It's all about first impressions and what a potential buyer sees when browsing through the Amazon store.

Sales, reviews, book covers – that's what counts, in that order.

NOTE: It's worth mentioning that if a book cover image does not reach the minimum 1000px size on its shortest side, there is a chance it will be de-ranked (see Amazon Seller guide), and even completely taken out of the ranking system.

Next, it's important to know which categories to place your book in. This is where most authors go wrong. When publishing an eBook in KDP (Kindle Direct Publishing), most authors will quickly select the first two eBook categories that seem the closest fit from the limited list of categories provided in KDP. **This is a BIG MISTAKE.**

Online shoppers at Amazon can discover books not only by entering keywords in the search box in Amazon, but also by searching through the Best Seller lists. Amazon has a "Top 100" list in hundreds of categories, and many readers will look at the best-selling books on page 1 and 2 of these Best Seller lists. Not only that, but based on the buyer's behavior, Amazon will send emails to the Amazon user recommending the Best Sellers in the categories she or he has been looking through. You really should be aiming to get your book to appear in these Best Seller lists to improve its visibility on Amazon. The more visible your book, the more likely you will get improved sales.

One of the first things you need to understand is that there is not just one Best Seller list on Amazon. Instead, Amazon divides all its books and eBooks into categories ranging from mainstream genres like Art and Photography to Travel. As our focus is mostly on eBooks, these are the main categories under Kindle eBooks:

Arts & Photography (142,429)
Biographies & Memoirs (113,515)
Business & Investing (154,352)
Children's eBooks (129,570)
Comics & Graphic Novels (19,690)
Computers & Technology (44,653)
Cookbooks, Food & Wine (36,470)
Crafts, Hobbies & Home (48,222)
Education & Reference (155,935)
Foreign Languages (553,537)
Gay & Lesbian (24,614)
Health, Fitness & Dieting (158,927)
History (139,199)
Humor & Entertainment (70,175)
Literature & Fiction (836,959)
Mystery, Thriller & Suspense (146,332)
Nonfiction (1,471,185)
Parenting & Relationships (50,171)
Politics & Social Sciences (175,917)
Professional & Technical (198,102)
Reference
Religion & Spirituality
Romance (181,050)
Science & Math (149,487)
Science Fiction & Fantasy (161,223)
Self-Help (65,392)
Sports & Outdoors (43,354)

Teen & Young Adult (52,560)
Travel (39,314)

NOTE: Amazon continuously changes these main categories, but generally the list I provide here is largely accurate.

This is a list I took from Amazon some time ago, so it could have changed a little, especially the numbers, which indicate the number of books in each category. In theory, the categories with the most books are the most competitive, which means it is hardest to rank highly in those categories since there are more books you need to rank higher than. But this is just a theory, because each mainstream category can have many sub-categories, and they in turn can have more sub-sub-categories... and so forth.

A sub-sub category in Travel could have fewer books than a sub-sub category in History, and therefore be less competitive. So, you really need to dig deep into the different categories on Amazon to understand the overall structure. Figuring all this out can take a very long time... but wait! The real shocker is that KDP, the channel you use to publish and describe your books, does not use these same categories as the ones displayed on the Amazon store. What?!! I really am not kidding you. It's true. So, if you just don't want to get into this quagmire of figuring out the best categories for your book, just ask for help from experts such as at kbookpromotions.com, who can figure all this out for you.

What is the point of an author using the book categories listed in KDP? Well, that's a good question since they don't match the book categories displayed on the Amazon website. Instead, Amazon uses "browser categories", which are very different and much more numerous than the ones shown in KDP.

Yet the secret to ensuring your book becomes an Amazon Best Seller, and perhaps even reaches #1, is to understand the book categories. Keep your thinking cap on, because the following is important.

I've just explained that the book categories on the Amazon

website do not match the categories listed in KDP. Let's now put ourselves in the shoes of the online visitor at Amazon to illustrate this more clearly. Visit the Amazon website and look for books there that you feel are similar to your own. They could be considered competitors if your book is in non-fiction, or covering the same theme if your book is fiction. Click on one and scroll down until you see the Product Details section. Below this you can see the book's Amazon Best Seller Ranking, such as in the example below:

Amazon Best Sellers Rank: #10,399 Paid in Kindle Store
#842 in Kindle Store > Kindle eBooks > Mystery, Thriller & Suspense > **Suspense**
#999 in Books > Mystery, Thriller & Suspense > Thrillers & Suspense >**Suspense**
#7083 in Books > **Literature & Fiction**

Just below the Amazon Best Sellers Rank, it shows your Amazon Sales Rank in the (usually) three most relevant book categories you have given for your book.

NOTE: More recently, Amazon has started shortening the way it displays categories so that, for example, it displays: #842 in <u>Suspense Thrillers</u> instead of:
#842 in Kindle Store > Kindle eBooks > Mystery, Thriller & Suspense > **Suspense**
So the full path appears hidden, but if you click on the shortened link <u>Suspense Thrillers</u> it will display the Best Sellers in that category and still display the full path on the left and side.

If you have a printed book, it will show a "Books" main category. If you have an eBook published in KDP, it will show a "Kindle Store > Kindle eBooks" main category.

In most cases, two Kindle eBook categories will be displayed, but if the author or publisher has failed to give more than one eBook category in KDP, then only one will be displayed – as is the case in the previous example. As we will see, authors who fail to give at least two eBook categories are making a big mistake, since they are potentially losing out on having their book appear in multiple Best Seller lists if their book does reasonably well.

If you next click on one of these Kindle eBook categories (such as "Suspense"), it will display the Top 100 Paid Best Sellers in "Suspense". It usually displays the first top 20 on the first page, so you can see the #1 best-selling book for this category at the very top left, and in sequence, the #2 and #3 (and so on) best sellers. If you then click on any of these books, you will see in their Product Details their Amazon Best Sellers Rank. For example:

Amazon Best Sellers Rank: #1,869 Paid in Kindle Store
#1 in Kindle Store > Kindle eBooks > Mystery, Thriller & Suspense > **Suspense**

This means that to get to the #1 spot in this book category, you are going to have to get an Amazon Best Sellers Rank of #1,868 or better. The lower the rank, the more sales this book is getting. Now do the same for books ranked #2 and #3, and you will see what you need to score to beat these competitors or rival authors in this category. I recommend you also look at book #20 in this same category. Most Amazon visitors will probably look at page 1 and page 2 of the Top Best Seller lists, but not much further. So, #20 is the easiest option to compete against to get decent visibility for your book. The book at #20 might look like this:

Amazon Best Sellers Rank: #4,009 Paid in Kindle Store
#20 in Kindle Store > Kindle eBooks > Mystery, Thriller & Suspense > **Suspense**

OK – from this investigation you have done of the top Best Seller books in your category, you can see that the lower the Amazon Best

Sellers Rank is, the higher you get in the Amazon Best Seller lists. You have also seen that, in this case, you need an Amazon Best Seller Rank of #4,008 to get into the Top 20 Paid Best Sellers in the category "Suspense".

The next question is, what does it take to get a Best Seller Rank of #4,008 so that you can get your book into the #20 spot in this category? Or if you are really ambitious and you want to be #1 in your book category, how can you get a lower Amazon Best Seller Rank of #1,869 in the category "Suspense"?

SPECIAL NOTE: The numbers I give below are at the time of writing this sentence. The numbers change frequently on Amazon, sometimes every hour, so please do your own research and check out the latest numbers in your book categories.

The answer is sales, and while the exact sales number you need to beat these competitors varies a little from one researcher to another, you can use the following as a general guide. This was provided by Amazon themselves at:

http://kdpcalculator.com/index.php - they have since taken the list down:

- Rank / Sales per day
- 1,000 / 100-300
- 2,000 / 55-100
- 3,000 / 30-55
- 4,000 / 10 to 30
- 5,000 / 10 to 30
- 6,000 / 10 to 30
- 7,000 / 10 to 30
- 8,000 / 10 to 30
- 9,000 - 40,000/ 1 to 10

It's not clear why Amazon took this calculator down, but from my experience, it was because it underestimated the sales numbers per day.

Another gentleman came out with this simpler calculation:

$$100,000/\text{rank \#} = \text{sales per day}$$

Several authors, such as Kimberlay Rae, have also provided their calculations, and most don't quite tally with others. At kbookpromotions.com, we know the number of purchases our subscribers make for a certain book each day, and frankly, that's the only way to do it: using fresh and reliable data. There are some secrets that I have to keep to myself and my clients, so all I will say here is that most calculations underestimate the sales per day needed to achieve a certain rank.

That said, the guidelines provided by Amazon earlier on are a decent rule of thumb for you to use. If you find it unreliable in your genre, then contact me.

So, you now know how many sales you need to get into the Best Seller lists for your book category. If the book you are trying to compete against looks like the example we showed earlier (#4,009 Paid in Kindle Store and #20 in Kindle Store > Kindle eBooks > Mystery, Thriller & Suspense > **Suspense**), then to get a rank of around #4,000, you need to sell about 10 to 30 books a day. Remember, this is the number Amazon has calculated for us.

Most authors want to be #1 in their category, or at least feature as highly in the ranking as possible. So, let's look at the example we gave earlier on:

Amazon Best Sellers Rank: #1,869 Paid in Kindle Store
#1 in Kindle Store > Kindle eBooks > Mystery, Thriller & Suspense >
Suspense

Using the Amazon KDP Calculator, this would require over 100 sales of your book per day.

That might be a number most authors cannot achieve, let alone maintain over a number of consecutive days, so the next question is, "How do I know if this is the best category for my book?" Or maybe, "Is there an easier book category for me to compete in so that I can get into the Best Seller charts on Amazon?"

Well, here it gets interesting. It's an area of much debate, but my advice is as follows:

1. Pick fights you think you can win
2. Aim for an eBook category where (to get into the Top 20) you need an Amazon Sales Rank lower than #15,000

Why? Well, let's look at each of these. It does not take long to realize that some eBook categories are much tougher to compete in than others. Romance, Mystery, Thriller, and Science Fiction are generally areas that sell well. Even if you dig deeper into each of these categories, you will see that some of its sub-categories are more popular than others. Let's take this example in the category Kindle Store > Kindle eBooks > Mystery, Thriller & Suspense.

Here I found an author ranking at #6. Her Amazon book page displays:

Amazon Best Sellers Rank: #669 Paid in Kindle Store
#6 in Kindle Store > Kindle eBooks > Mystery, Thriller & Suspense >
Crime Fiction > **Serial Killers**
#26 in Kindle Store > Kindle eBooks > Mystery, Thriller & Suspense
> Suspense > **Psychological**
#35 in Kindle Store > Kindle eBooks > Mystery, Thriller & Suspense
> Thrillers > **Crime**

Looking at the table provided by the Amazon KDP Calculator, I would not want to compete with this author. To rank at #669, you need big-time sales. This is not a fight I would want to compete in.

Now let's look at a slightly more niche area. One of the authors I promote writes Financial Thrillers. So, let's look here:

Amazon Best Sellers Rank: #14,977 Paid in Kindle Store (See Top 100 Paid)
#20 in Kindle Store > Kindle eBooks > Mystery, Thriller & Suspense > Thrillers > **Financial**

Hmmm... now this is more achievable. I need a rank of #14,977 or better to get to #20. This is about 10 sales a day, if we use Amazon's KDP Calculator table. So, this is a category I would recommend since you have a much better chance of making it to the Best Seller lists.

I also advised you to aim for an eBook category where the Amazon Sales Rank (to get into the top 20) is higher than #15,000. Why #15,000? Well, that's equivalent to 1 to 10 sales a day. This seems achievable, and not a bad sales figure to aim for (at least, to start with). Remember, staying ranked in the Best Seller lists means more visibility of your book on Amazon, and the better chance of visitors seeing your book and buying it. This is worth aiming for. So, if your book is a financial thriller, the above category I gave is the one for you.

What about going even more niche? What about going deep down into eBook categories where I could be #1 for just 5 sales a day? Should I try this? Well, there's good and bad news here. Let's start with the bad. Do you really want to be in such a small niche where so few buyers exist and where the average sales are possibly 5 to 20 books a week? Probably not, unless it's a really good fit for your book. However, here comes the good news, if your book does really well in this sub-sub category, Amazon will automatically rank your book in the parent category. Take the example of a relatively niche category of "Best Sellers in Work-Related Health" at:

Kindle Store > Kindle eBooks > Health, Fitness & Dieting > Personal Health > **Work-Related Health**

If your book does very well in this category, it will start to appear in its parent category:

Kindle Store > Kindle eBooks > Health, Fitness & Dieting > Personal Health

You can effectively double your chances by picking niche categories. Whatever doubts you might have about niche categories, they have several advantages. Your book reaching #1 in a small niche might well get you more visibility than being #87 in a more difficult category, and (as we have just seen) your book will be promoted up the parent category ranks if it does particularly well.

Now it's time to reveal one of those gems or "Amazon secrets" that you really need to know about.

Most of the sub-categories in the "browser categories" displayed on the Amazon website are not categories you can select within KDP.

You heard right. Amazon doesn't allow you to select most of the categories displayed on its website. As a result, most authors are competing in "super-categories", where you're pitted against the big guys: the big publishers who also don't know the ins-and-outs of KDP, so select the first categories that come to mind when they look at the options.

To select one of these sub-categories, you need to carry out one simple action: contact Amazon support and ask them to change your category. It's that easy. If, for some reason, you have a problem, just contact me. I have a standard email template that never fails in getting Amazon Support to change your eBook categories to the ones you want.

SPECIAL NOTE: As this book is about marketing your book and not how to publish it, I am assuming that you already know about how to publish your book in KDP (Kindle Direct Publishing) and know where to find the areas in it where you can define your book title, author name, and extras such as keywords and book categories. If not, please read up on it (there are many decent Kindle books on the subject) or research it using the KDP Help pages.

The next little gem I want to share with you is knowing the best possible eBook categories for your book. Which eBook category should I ask Amazon Support to change for my book? **Previously you could only select two eBook categories, but now Amazon allows up to 10 categories**, so it deserves some careful thought. Are there some other book categories I could add to make my book more visible on Amazon? You bet there is! And are there other categories where your book would rank higher in the Amazon Best Seller lists? Almost certainly.

NOTE: We are now treading in real "Amazon expert" territory here. Please skip the rest of this chapter unless you really want to dig deeper.

You can either spend hours, days, even weeks trawling through all the Amazon eBook categories... or simply ask an Amazon expert within our team at kbookpromotions.com. We've been studying this for years, and advising large number of our customers on the best book categories for their needs. The other alternative is to use some tools to help you select a category, but our experience in using them ourselves is that they don't have a broad enough view of all the hundreds of categories to find the best option. They can perhaps tell you that "Kindle Store > Kindle eBooks > Health, Fitness & Dieting

> Personal Health" is an easier option than "Kindle Store > Kindle eBooks > Health, Fitness & Dieting > Women's Health", but not tell you that there is a much better category for your book in a very different category area.

Here is a good example: An author who wrote mysteries of a religious nature asked for my help with book categories. Now, most people would clearly put this in the "Mystery, Thriller & Suspense" section of Amazon, perhaps:

Kindle Store > Kindle eBooks > Mystery, Thriller & Suspense > Mystery > Cozy

To get into the Top 20 Best Seller list, you would need an Amazon Best Sellers Rank of #1,026 in the Paid in Kindle Store. Ouch! That's very competitive, needing big sales.

Yet if he selected a sub-category in Literature & Fiction, such as "Kindle Store > Kindle eBooks > Literature & Fiction > Religious & Inspirational Fiction > Mystery", he just needs an Amazon Best Sellers Rank: of #12,429 to get to #1. Wow, that's a big difference. It's a good fit and has a much better chance of getting him into the #1 Best Seller spot.

Remembering that an author can select eight to ten book categories, this author added one sub-category under the Mystery, Thriller & Suspense, and the "Religious & Inspirational Fiction > Mystery" category I suggested to him, and it paid off! Not only did he rank much higher than he had before, but he actually doubled his chances of finding new readers since he can now attract readers in both the "Mystery, Thriller & Suspense" genre and the "Literature & Fiction > Religious & Inspirational Fiction" genre.

So, congratulations, you've now discovered what it takes to get your book into the Best Seller lists on Amazon! You've also learnt a secret or two about what you need to get there and the best way to select the best eBook category for your book. In effect, I've shared with you the fast and easy way to make your book into a Best Seller on Amazon, and gain extra visibility for your book you would not have gained otherwise.

Calculating your sales per day – a warning

Before we move on to other methods of making your book more visible on Amazon, I wanted to give you a cautionary note about tables and tools you may find on the internet that convert an author's Amazon KDP Best Seller rank into Kindle sales per day. Earlier on, I gave you the figures Amazon provided through its KDP Calculator Tool and other ways people calculate sales per day based on Amazon Sales Ranking.

I also warned that most of these tools and tables tend to underestimate the sales you need to achieve such ranks. So, do take care with tools and tables that give you exact figures. It just isn't that simple. Amazon Sales Ranking is affected by many factors, such as how many sales you got the day before or even several days before. It is also affected by how well your competitors are doing on a particular day within your book category. An Amazon Sales Rank can even be very different if you check it at 12 noon and then check it again at 6pm. The Ranking changes regularly, nearly every hour.

SPECIAL NOTE: It's worth noting that the A9 algorithm used by Amazon claims to update in real time. It could be that the sales index takes a while to run through but the actual engine should update as soon as a sale is made, in theory. There's nothing within the code to suggest it would need any sort of refresh.

Similarly, be cautious of tools that show you how many sales you can earn in a week or month for a certain eBook category. Many of these tools simply use "sales per day" tables (like the ones we have already looked at), and then multiply it by 30 to give you the money you could earn per month. So, if you can earn $50 a day in one category, it will tell you that you can earn a credible $50 x 30 = $1500 a month!

So, what's wrong with this? Well, as most authors who track their Amazon Sales Ranking regularly will tell you, your Amazon Sales Ranking does not stay constant each day. If your Ranking is #1,005 on Monday, it could be down to #21,680 by the following day. So, yes, it's far more unpredictable to work out how much money you could earn in each category.

Because of this, do carry out your own research and use any example "sales per day" tables you might find from other sources or other authors. Better yet, use the data in your own KDP Reports to validate the data you get, or contact me at kbookpromotions if you are really struggling with this and need more accurate estimates.

In the end, if getting on the Best Seller lists in your book category does not bring long-term revenue, it will gain you more visibility and credibility for your book, whether that is to impress potential publishers, to sooth your own ego, or to find new readers in your niche market. And if the Amazon sales machinery does its own stuff, it might just bring you the extra rise in sales you were hoping for.

CHAPTER 10

HOT NEW RELEASES

ANOTHER GREAT PLACE TO have your book appear in is Amazon's Hot New Releases. When I mention this to some authors, they ask, "Isn't this where all the latest blockbuster novels from big authors like John Green, Rick Riordan, Dean Koontz, and John Green appear? There's no chance of getting my book here, is there?"

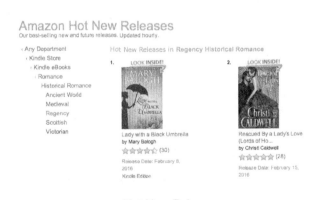

Hot New Releases

Of course there is! It's just a matter of understanding how Amazon works here, and the benefits of doing so are clear. Having your book appear in the Hot New Releases is like having your book advertised on a big banner in flashing bright lights on Amazon. Thousands of potential buyers look through the Hot New Releases, and Amazon promotes them through emails to buyers who have purchased books from the same category. You probably get these types of email promotions from Amazon too, right?

Just look at this email I just got from Amazon:

Subject: Hot New Releases in Biographies & Memoirs

"Richard,
We thought you might be interested in the following Hot New Releases in Biographies & Memoirs"

And there it provides links to the latest hot releases.

And these emails from Amazon really work! Their conversion rates are high, simply because many people getting these emails think, "Hey, it's just a few more bucks. Why not?" and click on that link to make that extra purchase.

Amazon even will entice readers to subscribe to these types of hot new releases. Here's another email I got last week from them.

Subject: New Release from {authorname}

"Richard,
You have subscribed to new release emails for {authorname}. You won't want to miss this new book."

Clearly, Amazon is trying its best to get readers to buy New Releases, whether they are Hot or just from an author whose book you have previously bought. So, the next question is, "How can I get my book into these Hot New Releases?" It's actually not as difficult as you might think.

How to get your book into Hot New Releases

Any book published recently (usually in the last 30 days) that appears in the Best Seller lists for a certain book category will also appear in the Hot New Releases section of Amazon. This is usually found just to the right of the Best Seller list. That's right, this is the way you can score a double whammy when you plan a book launch. I've shown you how to get into the Best Seller lists on Amazon, so just apply the same method to a book you have recently published in KDP, and your book will also appear as a Hot New Release.

Voilà – there you have it.

But what about books you have already published? Can they appear in the Hot New Releases? Strictly speaking, no, but there are several "black hat" marketing tricks you can learn to make your book more visible on the Amazon website. It's a bit like giving in to "the dark side" (if you are a Star Wars fan) or siding with Voldemort (if you like Harry Potter books), so I leave these sorts of methods to your own conscience. So, when an author asks me, "Is there a way to get into the Hot New Releases for a book I have already written some time ago?", I hesitate before I answer, "Yes, there are ways - If you only knew the power of the dark side." Sorry, I got carried away there; time to put my light saber away.

So, yes, there are ways. For example, ask yourself what would happen if you just republished your book again under a new date and number in KDP? Wouldn't Amazon therefore treat your book as a new publication? Yes, it would.

However, do take care with such "black hat" tricks. There is no escape from the dark side once you have entered it (there I go again). I would not recommend you using a new ASIN number for your book.

If you do this, yes, it will be treated as a new book, but as a consequence, you will lose all its history, including all the customer reviews you may have collected up until this point. So be careful what you wish for. Just remember what happened to Jafar at the end of Disney's Aladdin:

Aladdin: You wanted to be a genie? You got it!
[*Cuffs form on Jafar's wrists*]
Jafar: What?
Aladdin: And everything that goes with it.
[*Aladdin holds up a black genie lamp, which sucks Jafar in*]
Jafar: No! No!
Iago: I'm getting out of here!
Aladdin: Phenomenal cosmic powers...
[*Iago tries to flee, but Jafar grabs him*]
Iago: Come on, you're the genie. I don't want, I don't...!
[*both Jafar and Iago disappear in the lamp*]
Aladdin: ...in an itty-bitty living space.

So, be careful about being sucked in to these black-hat marketing techniques. They can be powerful, but only if you are fully aware of their consequences.

And then there was the author who wrote back to me saying, "Hey, is this a way to remove bad reviews of my book by simply republishing my book under a new ASIN?" Oh, boy, like I said before, "There is no escape from the dark side once you have entered it."

CHAPTER 11

CUSTOMERS WHO BOUGHT THIS ITEM ALSO BOUGHT

THIS IS A VERY visible feature within the Amazon store, and probably one that is more influential than many might imagine. Amazon shows this feature because it knows that it works, noticing that readers tend to buy similar books, and books others are reading. After all, when it comes to making decisions and buying patterns, Amazon knows we behave like sheep, following the rest of the herd.

You've no doubt seen this in many bookshops, too. They will list the top 20 best- selling books. But why should they do this if readers have a mind of their own and purchase the genres and novelists they are interested in? Well, that's because most book buyers in stores don't entirely have minds of their own. We don't enter a bookshop with a mission to buy a specific book. Well, very rarely. Instead we go in to browse and see what tickles our fancy and, yes, we often pick the books the majority of other readers are buying – the Best Sellers. Many of these might be Best Sellers simply because they were bundled into "2 for 3" bargain offers, so they are there because they are cheap rather than good. Whatever the reason, Amazon knows this and uses every trick in the book to try and get you to buy on their online store.

So, what can you do to get your book also featured in the "customers who bought this item also bought" areas of the Amazon website?

Customers Who Bought This Item Also Bought

Between Heartbeats
› Donelle Knudsen
⭐⭐⭐⭐☆ 15
Kindle Edition
$2.99

Court of Nightfall (The Nightfall Chronicles Book 1)
› Karpov Kinrade
⭐⭐⭐⭐☆ 325
Kindle Edition

Hidden Scars
Amanda King
⭐⭐⭐⭐⭐ 47
Kindle Edition
$2.99

Customers Who Bought …Also Bought

The answer is incredibly simple: get people to buy your book as well as the book you want your book to appear next to in the "Customers Who Bought This Item Also Bought" section. You require two actions here – first, you figure out which books you want to target, and second, you get a group of people to buy both books. In my experience, it takes about 4 to 7 days for the results to be updated on the Amazon website, so do wait a little time after the purchases have been made.

But what if you don't know of enough people to buy both books at the same time? Of course, this is when you need help from reader groups such as at kbookpromotions. Some might argue it's slightly unethical to control the results of Amazon in this way. Others might argue it's just salesmanship, using all your wits and resources to promote your book. Publishers use these types of tactics, so why not self-published authors?

The next question is, "How many people do I need to buy both these books for this to take effect on the Amazon website?" This is a little trickier, but by looking at the Amazon Sales Rank of the book you are targeting over the last few days (yes, there are tools that can do this for you), you can pretty much work out which of the books you wish to target are the easiest to influence, and how many books sales you need for each.

I have been quite amazed by how easy this is to do, and many of the authors I have helped with this task have been more than delighted by the results. After all, even if there is no real way to measure how many sales you get from it, just to see your book next to a famous author or novel is worth a lot in itself. If you are a writer of fictional spy novels, imagine your book appearing alongside classic fictional characters like James Bond or newer hotshots like Jason Bourne and Jack Ryan. Or if you write cookbooks, imagine your book alongside famous TV chefs like Jamie Oliver, Rachel Ray, or Heston Blumenthal. Imagine no longer, because with this feature within Amazon, you can make it happen.

CHAPTER 12

MOVERS AND SHAKERS

I CONSIDER the Movers and Shakers list on Amazon to be the icing on the cake, or rather the icing on the Best Sellers Lists. It is probably the hardest list to join, and therefore, the most influential.

This is an extremely difficult list to get into since it has no book categories at all. It is simply a list of the Top 400 most sold books in the whole Kindle Store in the last 24 hours.

To get into this list, you are talking about making thousands of sales a day. It ranks books by how much they have gone up the Amazon Sales Ranking ladder. So, a book that has jumped from a rank of #540 to #1 in the Amazon Sales Ranks will not feature as highly as a book that has jumped from a rank of #82,000 to #230. As the title suggests, Movers and Shakers list the books that have moved the most in the last 24 hours.

To have any chance of getting on this list, you really need a very aggressive launch plan, or a very large existing reader base to promote to. Few authors can muster the thousands of books that need to be sold here. Interestingly, it is based just on the Amazon Sales Rank, so books sold at $0.99 tend to be more common here than books sold at higher prices. A tactic many authors use is to offer a new book (as part of their book launch) at a reduced price of $0.99 and include some other value add-ons. Yet because we are dealing with the very best selling Top 400 books across all of the Kindle Store, most authors will never make it onto this list.

The good news is that there is another list that is also influential in getting visibility for your book and which is far more attainable.

CHAPTER 13

POPULARITY LISTS

APPEARING in Popularity Lists can have a big influence on the sales of your book, and is far more achievable than making it to the Movers and Shakers list on Amazon.

The Popularity Lists, like the Best Seller Lists, uses the "browser categories" employed by Amazon on its web store. For this reason, the two lists are often confused with each other, but they are quite different.

The easiest way to find them is by going to your home page in the Kindle Store and browsing the list of categories displayed on the left-hand side. Clicking on any of these categories will take you to the Popularity Lists. Here we begin to see why this list is different from the Best Seller Lists. For example, you will not see two different tabs separating Paid books from Free books. You might also notice that, unlike the Best Seller Lists, there is no "Top 100" listed here. In other words, Popularity Lists include ALL the books in that category across the whole Kindle Store.

So how does Amazon determine which are the most popular books in a particular category? It does this by counting the number of book sales and the number of downloads for a book, including free books, over a 30-day period.

Wow, now that's quite a different perspective on things, and one we have to factor in ourselves if we wish our book to be included in the Popularity Lists.

So, let's look at the criteria Amazon uses to determine which books make it to the Popularity Lists:

- It does not rank based on the Amazon Sales Rank of a book. In other words, it takes a wider perspective of overall sales, looking not at immediate sales of a book, but how it has generally performed over the last 30 days.
- The price of a book does count, so books sold at $2.99 will carry more weight than books at $0.99
- Free books that have been downloaded also count, but borrowed books (including from Kindle Unlimited) do not count.

There is a certain inconsistency here, because thousands of books are borrowed every minute on Amazon, yet Amazon has decided that this is not relevant in its calculation of what constitutes a popular book.

Now, let's stand back and look at the implications of this. The first and most obvious difference is the inclusion of free books. Given that readers often pick up free books ten times more often than discount or full-priced books, this must be taken into account. Your book could be selling 1000 copies in a month compared to a competitor that sold only 400 copies that month, but if that competitor also managed 5000 free downloads, then it could well end up being included in the Popularity List rather than yours.

Consider the following: if a book's popularity is decided by its performance over the last 30 days, it is likely to stay in its position longer than if it were in the Best Sellers List. Also, be aware that the

Popularity Lists are not updated as frequently, often only every 2 to 3 days.

So, to enter the Popularity Lists, you need a broader strategy than just getting your book into the Best Seller lists. Instead, you need to focus your efforts over a 30-day period, aiming for maximum sales and maximum downloads.

In general, I recommend you carry out the following three promotions over a 1-month period:

- A full price book promotion (targeting the Best Seller lists)
- A discount book promotion (offering your book at $0.99)
- A free book promotion (to get the maximum number of downloads)

It does not really matter in which order you run these three book promotions because the goal is to get the maximum number of sales and downloads of your book.

SPECIAL NOTE: Some book promoters argue that the order in which you promote your book does matter for your Amazon Sales ranking and other lists. The argument is that if one of Amazon's factors for exposure is price, then it is best to run the full price book first and then slash the price, and finally the free book offer.

For the full price book promotion, I would generally recommend pricing your book at $2.99 or $3.99 since this will earn you 70% royalty fees without putting off any prospective buyers based on price. The real problem with trying to get in the Popularity Lists is that there is no obvious score to beat. Recall that in the Best Seller lists, you can work out the specific Amazon Sales Rank you need to beat to get into the top 20 Best Seller lists for your category. As a result, it's really a case of putting all hands on deck, and giving it your best shot.

The discount book promotion also makes sense to carry out because you need to attract as many readers as possible, including those that look for bargain discount offers. By pricing your book at $0.99, you will only get 35% royalty on sales, but you will increase your overall sales during the 30 days – something the Popularity List will use to determine if your book will be included or not.

Then there is the free book promotion. These types of promotions are not attracting the mass numbers of a few years ago, but they can still bring in impressive numbers. I have helped promote free books that resulted in downloads of 1 to 10 thousand in a day. Yet other times, they have dribbled in at 100 or less a day. On the whole, it is well worth preparing for this, figuring out the best sites to advertise your book while it is free. Aim for at least 25 sites on which to promote your free book. You may have to consider paying a small fee for appearing on some of these sites.

Please be aware that there is no guarantee that such promotions will get you into the Popularity Lists. There remain several unknown factors. What is better, selling 50 books at $5.99 or 50 books at $2.99? Amazon does not let us entirely know.

SPECIAL NOTE: This is for the geeks among us who are prepared to try and understand Amazon's algorithm: According to certain sources, it is based on price-to-stock turnover, comparison of price to other products that are similar, and profit margins. As you cannot measure stock-to-price with an infinite stock, it is possible that 5.99 would be favored, but only in the case that books in your category are also 5.99, so this would indicate that 2.99 books would get more exposure due to collaborative filtering.

And then there is the unknown factor of how well your competitors in the same genre will do during those 30 days.

This is difficult to control and to predict, but without a broader strategy targeting maximum sales and downloads a month, you are certainly not likely to make it to the Popularity Lists.

CHAPTER 14

AMAZON'S SEARCH BOX

ANOTHER PLACE where you want your book to be found is in the Amazon search results. When people search for books or products on Amazon, they use the search box found near the top of most Amazon pages.

There is some debate at the moment on just how Amazon's search box works. I'll cover both schools of thought on this. The traditional view is that there are just two important mechanisms at play when Amazon's search engine displays its search results based on what you have typed into its search box.

- Its attempts to find the best matches by mapping your search words to keywords found in book titles, authors' names, subtitles, and the book's meta-data.
- Its autocomplete suggestions

The objective here is to ensure your book is listed near the top when people are searching on the Kindle Store. So, if someone types in the search word "Historical Romance", and you are an author of that genre, then you will want your book listed in the search results.

Using search words

The general advice offered by many eBook marketing pundits is to include your desired keywords in your book title, subtitle, and even book series and author name, but some of these suggestions go a little too far and are not practical for many authors. Yes, you can include keywords in your book title, but generally this is more useful for books of non-fiction than fiction. A book entitled "French Cookery: Top 100 Dishes" with the subtitle "French Cooking at its Best" is a good match for people searching for a book on "French cooking".

SPECIAL NOTE: Be careful of overplaying keywords in titles and subtitles. Amazon has started to indicate it will penalize books that go too far in this area.

However, I am less convinced that people use the Amazon search box to look for books of fiction. For example, how many of us search for books with keywords like "Historical Romance"? And even if we do, Amazon will most likely display the books in the browser category "Romance >Historical Romance" than any books with those words in their title.

For non-fiction books, especially, it's important to utilize the seven keywords Amazon KDP allows you to use in the meta-data fields of your book. These seven keywords should be selected with some due thought and research. Ensure they are relevant and popular keywords. Put yourself in the shoes of the prospective buyer of your book when browsing in the Kindle Store – what search words are they likely to use to find a good match to your book?

For example, if you have a book with the title "Tick Tock", and it's about making watches, it makes sense to include keywords like "watchmaking" in your book title. So, consider changing your book title to "Watchmaking: Tick Tock" with the subtitle "Watchmaking

Made Simple". In doing so, your book has a much higher chance of being displayed by Amazon when someone searches for "watchmaking".

Amazon's autocomplete suggestions

More likely than not, most potential buyers in the Kindle Store will find a book using the autocomplete suggestions from Amazon. This happens as you start typing a search word into the search box, only to be provided with a dropdown list box with multiple suggestions. This is Amazon's way, and a method used by many websites, to guide your search word selection by prompting you to use the most popular search words. Let's look at an example. If you type in the search word "historical", you will most likely be given popular search words like "historical fiction", "historical romance", or "historical fiction best sellers". If your original intention was to search for "historical romantic comedy", you might find yourself interrupted in the middle of your typing, and selecting "historical romance" instead. The autocomplete suggestions are therefore very important, since they clearly influence the potential buyer and the books that get displayed. The search words that come up in the auto complete suggestions might well be the ones you should target.

Amazon's Auto-Complete Suggestions

Black hat practices: There are a number of tricks authors use to try and influence the Amazon search engines. For example, I've seen many authors asking me to click on a link that contains their book title and keyword.

The syntax of the link would end along the lines of:

www.amazon.com/... keywords=Booktitle+romantic+comedy

So, if my novel had the book title "Breathless", and "romantic comedy" was a keyword I was trying to rank high on, then the link I would send people would end with:

www.amazon.com/... keywords=Breathless+romantic+comedy

If you are unsure of the exact link to send people, just go to the Amazon search box and enter the search words "yourbooktitle yourkeyword" and then copy the URL that Amazon generates and send it to others. It can be a rather long URL, so you can use tools like Bitly or Shorturl to shorten it.

The theory here is that the more people who use this search phrase, the higher your book will rank for that search word.

Sounds pretty convincing – right?

OK. Here's the catch. Most people don't even know how long it takes Amazon to refresh its search engine results to see if this technique really works. But I have further doubts about this idea. Assume a person used the search word "romantic comedy" and bought a competitor's book called "50 Shades of Pink and Blue", while 10 people you sent the link to clicked on it, but did not buy your book.

Which of the books do you think Amazon will rank higher? Your book that people visited 10 times and scored a big fat zero in sales, or the other book that just got 1 visitor but achieved an impressive 100% conversion rate to sale? Remember, Amazon is driven by sales. So... I think Amazon would favor your competitor's book. Wouldn't you?

I've yet to conduct a wide enough A/B test on this, but early tests I did with a group of other readers suggest that my suspicion is right on this one. So be careful when using such black hat tricks. It might be yourself you are fooling rather than the Amazon search engine. Simply try it out yourself and see if your ranking goes up, and for how long (1 hour, 1 day, 5 days?).

This takes me to the latest school of thought regarding how Amazon's search bar works. This one runs quite contrary to the traditional view and states that you cannot figure out keywords that people use to find your book by typing into the search bar and seeing what is autosuggested. Instead, it states that the results of the search bar are personalized to you and you alone.

So, the search bar is tailored to each individual user to show personalized product lists based on several factors, from the previous books you have purchased to specific products Amazon wants to push your way.

Let's look at an example I found on the Internet where a person states:

"I have had to buy a lot of Christian non-fiction to study certain buying behaviors for Christian author clients. As a result, I now have a purchase history that looks like I go to church and read about Christianity on a regular basis even though I don't. Because of this, I am now served suggestions such as "The Bible Diary 2016" maybe because I bought a diary recently also, and "Hymns for Women". I guess, because I am a woman."

So, when we use search words in the search bar, each of us will get largely different results. How does the search bar work then? Well, it seems that the results Amazon uses to autocomplete your search are based on the following:

- What you searched for previously
- What you browsed previously
- What you bought previously
- What other people who are similar in demographic bought before in the same basket
- What categories you search in more often
- Products that Amazon thinks you'd like to know about
- Social media use – Facebook for sure, probably Goodreads, and others that have not been confirmed yet
- IP address history
- GPS data from mobile
- What you've clicked on when Amazon recommended a product

In conclusion, we have some way to go before we fully understand how the search bar works in Amazon and how it can best be leveraged to your advantage. If you form your own opinion based on your own testing of the Amazon search bar, do let me know.

I am often asked how you can get your book to the top of Amazon's search results. Wouldn't that be great! Well, after further research and a number of promotional campaigns with other authors, I cracked the secret!. Here's the evidence:

My Book At The Top Of Amazon's Search Results

So, in this example, you can see in Amazon's search bar that the keyword "self-publishing" has been entered.

HINT: if reading this on your reader or iPad, you can click on the image to zoom in and read the text more easily.

And, lo and behold, my book is ranked #1 in Amazon's search results.

Getting your book to #1 on page 1 of Amazon's search results can be an amazing experience given the fierce competition you face, but it can be done!

How to achieve this needs some more detailed explanation and can be found in my other book "Self Publishing Disruption" and look up the chapter entitled "How to get your book to #1 of Amazon's search results".

CHAPTER 15

FINDING NEW READERS - OUTSIDE OF AMAZON

IN THE INTRODUCTION to this book, I commented on that eureka moment when I discovered that the best ways to promote books is within Amazon itself.

However, it would be a little remiss of me if I didn't comment on the other most popular ways of attracting new visitors outside of Amazon. I will not go into much detail about these, with the exception of book subscription services, which are a great way to advertise and promote your book.

Virtual blog tours, writing all your own blogs, tweeting on Twitter, and making friends on Facebook - all of these are good in their own way. For some authors, they can also help improve sales results. But be very careful with their "return rates". Earlier on in this book (The Good, The Bad, and The Ugly), I explained the shortcomings of such social media efforts. It simply supports the famous 80/20 Rule, first demonstrated by an Italian gentleman called Pareto. It particularly struck home for me when I read Perry Marshall's book "80/20 Sales and Marketing: The Definitive Guide to Working Less and Making More." The 80/20 Rule says:

"80 Percent of Your Results Come from 20 Percent of Your

Efforts, and 20 Percent of Your Results Come from The Other 80 Percent."

My suspicion is that much of the effort spent by authors to promote their books on social media represents the other part of this rule: the "20 percent of your results that come from the 80 percent" of your time.

Yet there are some areas outside of Amazon that are definitely worth leveraging. If you are going to concentrate on marketing activities outside of Amazon, these are the key activities to focus on.

The main one I want to cover is the use of book subscription services. I have mentioned these before, but now it's time to look at them in more detail.

CHAPTER 16

BOOK SUBSCRIPTION SERVICES

BOOK SUBSCRIPTION SERVICES (or book promotion sites) are considered by many to be the best way to advertise and promote your books.

In an earlier chapter, I explained why they were the "Good" in "The Good, The Bad, and The Ugly" of eBook marketing. This is because most of the reliable ones can be trusted to deliver very positive results and even be contacted for any additional questions you might have.

Before we look into each of these book promotion providers, let's momentarily go back to the eBook Marketing Magic Quadrant I introduced earlier on. Not all advertisers will provide a good experience. So, remember to look at the ones that deliver the highest value to you in the Magic Quadrant. Look for the ones that can deliver the best revenue and the most engaged readers. Even better, look out for the ones that provide reliable if not guaranteed results. If you're not sure, try their cheaper packages before spending more on them. Build trust and confidence with them.

Trust is very important. That's why I like the author at the Kindle

Books and Tips blog site who tells it to you the way it really is when it comes to advertising. Here's what he has to say:

"Thank you for your interest in advertising.

Your book's particulars will be sent out to just over 675,000 enthusiastic Kindle readers, including

- 600,000+ people accessing the blog via the free reader app or the Collections app for their Kindle Fire.

- 150,000+ people via an e-Ink Kindle subscription, email or social media subscription, or directly on the blog's website, or via an RSS reader.

Let's be honest about web marketing. While the above numbers look impressive I am not going to try and fool you, as the reality is although each day's posts go out to over 750,000 people approximately 100,000 people take action (i.e., read a particular day's post); it also does not mean I am implying 100,000 people will buy your book. I'd rather be upfront with you about circulation numbers as I'm not aware of, for example, any Kindle-focused website truly delivering 100% of their hundreds of thousands of Facebook followers for daily posts."

Many advertisers will try to impress you with their huge lists of subscribers, but do not be blinded by large numbers. It's quality that counts, not quantity.

OK - let's now look at the book subscription services that are among the most popular, and for good reasons. For this summary, I'd like to refer to a company that has carried out quite extensive tests on many book promotion sites, and that is from PaidAuthor who listed the "Best Book Promotion Sites 2019" on their website at:

www.paidauthor.com/best-ebook-promotion-sites

The list is too large to repeat here and gets updated quite regularly, so the best bet is for you to go there and check out the names there.

Many of the same top promoters also appear in a survey carried out by KindleBookReview, so getting a recommendation from two separate sources can only be a good thing. This survey is quite detailed and can be found at:

www.kindlebookreview.net/docs/top5bookpromoters_survey2.pdf

This survey, although a little older now, provides a number of interesting insights into the best ways self-published authors should be promoting their eBooks. Over 300 self-published authors participating in the survey and were asked an interesting series of questions ranging from the best places to seek book reviews to how much money authors spend on promoting their books each year.

The main conclusions from the survey were:

- The majority of authors (68%) recommend using book promotion services to advertise their book
- 43% of authors in the survey often or occasionally use book promotion services to gain sales, downloads, reviews of their books
- The top 5 recommended promotional services all scored over 60% in being "strongly recommended" or "recommended" by the authors in the survey.
- The top 5 recommended book promotional services were BookBub, KindeBookPromotions, Ereadersnewstoday, Kindlenationdaiily.com, Bargainbooksy.com. Honorable mentions also went out to BookGorilla, Pixel of Ink, and FreeBookSys.

NOTE: I was one of the sponsors of this survey, so be cautious of surveys sponsored by vendors, but generally the survey is very interesting in seeing the emerging trends in how authors are promoting their books.

In reality, there is no one shoe that fits the needs of all authors. One promotion site may work well for one author, but not so well for another. So it really is a case of trial and error, looking up the profile of each promoter and trying out the ones that appeal the most to you. If one of them performs well in getting you good sales results and some reviews, then use them again. If you have a bad experience, then you probably won't want to use them again.

For good reasons, the more expensive services are usually the ones that deliver the best results. They are under heavy demand, so they charge more. BookBub is the classic example of this, charging over $2000 for a number of their promotions. So let's now look at the best ways to ensure these services accept your book.

Many of them have waiting lists due to their popularity, and consequently have strict criteria for the books they decide to promote. To get the best out of these services and be accepted by them, please follow these next top tips:

1. First, consider what your goal is before using any of these services. Take your time to analyze the benefits of each service, and ask yourself which ones come closest to what you are seeking: More sales? More reviews? More visibility?
2. Provide the information they ask for, and try not to cut and paste standard replies you already have. Each service should be treated individually and your answers personalized so that they clearly see you seriously want their services.
3. Do not use multiple book subscription services at the same time. This is tempting to do if you want maximum impact for a book launch, but it will result in you not

being able to easily tell which of the services actually performed the best, and delivered on what they promised.

4. Have a clear idea on the promotion dates you would like to use for each service. In most cases, you'll want a promotion date a few weeks after your submission. But state that you are flexible on the promotion dates. This will enable them to more easily fit your book into their already busy promotional calendar.

5. Make sure you keep track of the promotion dates you requested, and ensure you have access to your KDP (Kindle Direct Publishing) so you can verify the results they get for you.

6. Most services require a payment through PayPal, so ensure you have a PayPal account set up beforehand. Make sure you know the email address associated with your PayPal account.

7. Take care with free promotions. As covered in this book, they have some advantages and disadvantages. Authors with multiple books will have a better chance of leveraging a free promotion, but the days of expecting high sales of your other books after a free promotion are quickly disappearing. Free book promotions are very useful if you are planning to get on the Amazon Popularity Lists (see "Popularity Lists" covered elsewhere in this book for details).

8. Learn to walk before you can run, meaning that it's better to invest a little first, and when you are happy with the results of the service, to spend more. This can be difficult with sites like BookBub, where they often allow you to promote your book only once, so taking care about how you spend your money is important.

9. If possible, look for services that provide guaranteed results, or provide a pro-rated refund service if they don't

get you the expected result. Be cautious of services that give you no indication of the sales results you will get.

10. Consult with other authors to find out what they have tried and what they recommend. While one service might work well for one author but not for another, recommended services generally perform better than most others.

CHAPTER 17

THE IMPORTANCE OF BOOK REVIEWS

WHILE NOBODY CAN EXACTLY EXPLAIN what makes one book commercially successful, and another not, there is a general consensus on the ingredients you need to have any chance of making your book sell well. The ingredients for long-term success of self-published books include:

- A professional-looking book cover
- A well-edited book
- A good number of decent reviews

If you were to examine most successful books that stay in the Best Seller lists for a good period of time, you will see that nearly all of them have high-star rated reviews, and a good number of them. If you then examine the reviews on Amazon, you will see that while many of these reviews are quite short and to the point, they do contain a good number of well-written reviews with a decent length of about 150 to 300 words. It is these reviews that often convince curious online shoppers to buy the book. Book reviews provide social proof, and most people make decisions by looking at what other people do.

So, it is clear that any author's marketing strategy should include the pursuit of reviews for their books, especially on Amazon, where people buy books with a mere click of a button. And it's not just about getting a few reviews, but a good number of them.

What is the best way to go about getting reviews? Well, the answer lies in the following message, and one I want you to remember:

IT'S NOT ABOUT GETTING REVIEWS; IT'S ABOUT FINDING REVIEWERS

For those in the publishing world, this should come as no surprise. If it works for publishers, who are the professionals in this industry of marketing and selling books, why should it not work for self-published authors, too?

All publishers recognize the power of reviews. For this reason, publishers send advance review copies (ARCs) to prospective readers to build momentum and enthusiasm for a book. They seek out the famous reviewers in news outlets like the New York Times, and the top 100 reviewers on Amazon. They will gladly pay for reviews from book review services such as Kirkus Reviews and several others. They will then include excerpts of these reviews in their advertising and promotional material. They will even include these reviews in the Editorial Review section on Amazon so that most prospective buyers will see it.

Reviews are clearly part of their strategy to sell books, so shouldn't it be yours, too? Whether it's for books, movies, theater shows, DVDs, or new computer games, professional organizations in the business of selling know that reviews help sell.

One has only to look at Amazon, the largest book retailer in the world and the way they elevate reviews on their website to see further confirmation of this. Just go and visit Amazon.com and look at the overall structure of a book page. If you are an author with a book already on Amazon, look for your book and you'll notice the summary of reviews displayed near the top of the page just below your name. This prominent position clearly indicates Amazon's view on how important reviews are in influencing visitors to buy a book.

Amazon also draws the visitor's attention to two key elements high up on the page: the star ranking and how many customer reviews a book has received. Many visitors will simply look at the number of stars a book has and the number of reviews a book has. Some buyers may not buy a book if the star rating is 3 or lower. Whether we like it or not, books with lots of reviews will attract the eye of the prospective buyer.

Amazon is clearly using reviews to measure the quality of a book and to entice readers to buy books. It's no coincidence that they place information about the reviews so high up on the page for all to see. It does this simply because it believes it's a good way to get more sales, and market research seems to support them in this belief.

For example, a study by the Yale School of Management carried out by Judith Chevalier and Dina Mayzlin ("The Effect of Word of Mouth on Sales: Online Book Reviews") examined the effect of consumer reviews on relative sales of books at Amazon.com and Barnesandnoble.com. They conclude that book reviews lead to an increase in relative sales.

"Moderating Roles of Review Credibility and Author Popularity on Book Sales", by Professor Xiao Ma, is a detailed independent research paper from Wisconsin School of Business, citing many surveys and studies from the last ten years. This impressive research paper also shows that reviews generate sales.

In many ways, these research papers just confirm what we intuitively already knew: reviews help generate book sales. So, to generate sales for your book, you need to consider the best ways to get book reviews.

But, boy, this can be difficult! The problem is that very few people who like your book will write and post a review. Think about your own experience. When was the last time you read a book, then went onto Amazon to post a review?

Michael Alvear (in his book "Making a Killing in Amazon") estimates that just 0.0002% of readers of one of the best-selling books will post a review. Other sources, such as Steve Levitt and Stephen Dubner (in their blog, Freakanomics) estimate that only 1 in a 1000 book purchases will result in a review!

Wow. That seems an incredible statistic. I'm more inclined to think that it's closer to 1 in 100, but either way, it's clear that getting book reviews is difficult.

The problem here is that these figures are based on authors using the usual methods of using social media and emails to any other people they might know to generare reviews for them.

While this sounds quite sensible, it simply does not work very well. Remember what I said about using social media to sell books, and the stats I provided?

This is the wrong approach!

As mentioned before, the secret is in finding reviewers, not reviews. Reviewers, by their nature, are simply much more likely to post a review of your book once they have read it. And there are far more reviewers out there than you might think.

Just look at the top 1000 reviewers on Amazon. If you were to examine their profiles and see the type of reviews they write, there is one thing that stands out. These people love to write reviews. Some of them write as many as ten to twenty reviews a day, and they clearly want to have their voices heard. They are simply a different kind of people from the rest of us. They are motivated to write reviews for their own reasons, and that's just fine - as long as they carry on writing reviews, because this is what you, I, and every author want from them.

In summary, we have shown clear evidence that reviews help generate sales. The market research shows this to be true, and whether we like it or not, it's Amazon's main method of helping potential readers to decide to buy a book.

Given the importance of getting book reviews, let me cover this subject in more detail by answering some of the most frequently asked questions I get on this topic.

Is getting a lot of book reviews important?

I've mentioned previously that it is important, but this depends a little on the type of book you are writing and its genre. Consider reviews as forming a kind of "social proof" that your book is worthy of being purchased by others. From this point of view, getting a decent volume of reviews is important for at least two important reasons.

Firstly, let's remember that shoppers are like sheep – they will follow the rest of the flock. Consider two similar books: one has 3 reviews, the other has 15 reviews. Which is the better book? Well, there's no real way of knowing without reading the books, but social proof shows that most of us will select the book with the most reviews. A book with just 3 or 4 reviews might indicate that it is not widely read, and might even raise the suspicion that the reviews may have come from the author's mother and some friends.

In contrast, if your book has lots of reviews, it indicates you have a decent volume of readers who like your book. It's difficult to know how many reviews you need, but some believe 50-plus reviews indicates it is read by the mainstream, and anything over 100 indicates you have a hot book that is selling well. If you get to thousands of reviews, well, then you are in Harry Potter land, and definitely rubbing shoulders with the other author giants on Amazon.

Not convinced yet about the number of reviews influencing the buyer? Well, let's look at this article I found on the Internet about one buyer's experience in deciding which book to buy on Amazon:

"I bought Ariely's book because my colleague Frank suggested it while we were chomping down some food. I think he mentioned the title just once. We didn't discuss it further, but it was just enough of a trigger that the next time I was on Amazon I looked up the title. That's when the 463 reviews convinced me to buy it, over all the alternatives."

Take notice. "I bought it, over all the alternatives", including the option of not buying anything at all. A lot of Amazon reviews makes buyers, and even non-buyers, buy.

Have you ever gone to a play and given a standing ovation at the end? You have, right? And chances are, you didn't start the standing ovation. It's unlikely you were even the third or fourth to stand. Chances are, you stood up and clapped like a seal only when it was clear that an ovation trend had started. This is the power of social proof.

Social proof is a hardwired "herd mentality" setting in our human makeup. When others do something, we automatically and subconsciously determine that it is safe and even in our best interest to do the same.

The book and product reviews on Amazon work the same way. The more reviews that people see for your product, the more likely they are to buy it. It triggers the social proof shortcut for your consumers. "Obviously, many others are buying it, so I will buy it. Even if it sucks."

So, there you have it: quantity counts.

The second interesting fact is that if you get a certain volume of reviews, more will most likely follow. There's a certain domino effect here, where reviews will beget reviews. It's no coincidence that when you analyze books with lots of reviews, many of them have 4 or 5 reviews from Vine or Top 500 Amazon Reviewers. It's almost as if when you get one top Amazon reviewer to write about your book, other top reviewers feel compelled to follow suit and write another review. It's as if they don't want to be left behind, and want to jump on the same bandwagon.

There you have it. In many cases, it's about which book is making the loudest noise that counts, and not about the specific content of a book. When an online shopper sees a book with lots of reviews and a decent star rating, then the buying decision is so much easier, and on Amazon, it takes just one click to make the purchase.

What is the best way to seek book reviews?

I've touched on this before, but it's worth repeating. I believe authors have approached this the wrong way. Influenced by articles they find on Google and discussions on social media sites, they follow the herd and copy what has been recommended. They are encouraged to find reviews by a multitude of methods that involve hours, even days, of time and effort interacting on social media, asking people to buy their books and post reviews on Amazon.

Authors are even asked to edit their book again to include headers and trailers in their book asking for reviews. Others are encouraged to contact other authors they know, or even friends and family to get these reviews. Unknown to them, some of these so-called best practices are actually against Amazon's review policy.

While all these efforts might generate a few reviews, the fundamental mistake is that authors should stop groveling for reviews from practically anybody. In fact, this can actually lead to a negative result by getting you a few reviews, but only bad ones. For example, this can happen when authors offer their books for free for a short period of time. The result is that many downloading the book will have done so simply because it was free. And it is during these free promotions that a small raft of 1-star or poorly written reviews will be posted.

The lesson here is to focus not on reviews, but on specific reviewers. Some of the reasons for this become pretty clear when you stop and have a good think about it. For example, you might think that family and friends might be the most likely to post reviews of your book on Amazon. Wrong! Firstly, Amazon does not approve of you asking family, or friends, or even authors you know to write reviews. If they discover this, they will remove the reviews. Secondly, many of your friends and family probably don't even know how to post reviews on Amazon. You'll be lucky to get even one of them to succeed.

On the other hand, if you look at Amazon's top reviewers and those who like to write book reviews on their blogs, you will see that they write reviews on a very regular basis. For them, writing reviews in no burden. They actually LIKE to do it. Even if you look at the reviewers outside the top 1000 reviewers on Amazon, or look in certain online book niches, you'll find people who post reviews regularly.

The point is that there are two kinds of people in this world when it comes to book reviews: those that are likely to write reviews, and those that are not. Begging and screaming for reviews from the latter group is like hitting your head against a brick wall.

In my early days of promoting books, I once sold over 3000 books for an author I was helping to promote, even offering the book for free for a short period of days. We included all the tricks and best practices of asking for reviews. The result? We got one review, and a poor one at that, consisting simply of 5 words.

I won't repeat the 5 words since they were pure trash and clearly showed they hadn't gone beyond the first 10 pages before posting their review.

So, it's all about finding the first category of readers we mentioned: the reviewers.

What's the best way to find reviewers?

One option is to find the reviewers yourself, but this takes a great deal of time and effort. It certainly is an option, but you need more than this if you don't yet have a large email list of readers who have read your books in the past.

In my opinion, book subscription services are the best way to do this, or the use of tools that help you data-mine Amazon in seeking out reviewers. Let's look at each of these in turn.

For book subscription services, look for the ones that can find readers in a specific genre – your genre. The vendors that stand out here are BookBub, ENT, and kbookpromotions.

BookBub and ENT will get you some reviews simply due to the sheer volume of readers they have. The plan is that by promoting your book to hundreds, if not thousands, of readers in your genre, a number of them will write reviews. The main issue here is that these types of promotions are for readers, and not specifically aimed at reviewers. There is also the risk mentioned earlier that if you run a free promotion, it might solicit some bad reviews, so go for discounted book offer promotions here if possible, if your goal is to get reviews.

On the other hand, kbookpromotions does specifically target reviewers. As a result, the audience numbers here are smaller in volume, but far more focused. Like BookBub and the other popular book subscription services, kbookpromotions will send a promotional email to readers who like the same genre as your book.

So how do these book promoters find these reviewers? Well, this brings me to the other option I mentioned of using software tools that can data-mine the Amazon websites.

For a while now, there have been tools you can purchase that analyze books on Amazon.com. Most of them focus on finding keywords for your book by looking at similar books in your category, or by trying to estimate how much money you could make in other book categories. A few of these tools go a bit further and can even crawl through all the reviews written in a certain book category and extract emails if the reviewers have left them in their reviewer profile.

Now, using screen-scraping tools could work for you, but it still does take a great deal of time and effort even after you have scraped a list of emails together. Firstly, not all the emails you extract will work (since some may be rather old), and not all the people you email will respond to your request to write a review. In many ways, it's a numbers game – the more email addresses you get, the bigger the chance of getting more reviews. Contacting the reviewers yourself by email can be a heavy burden on your time, but by trial and error, you can get there in the end.

What's the best way to get positive reviews for my book?

Yes, of course it's great to get positive reviews, but it's far better to get honest reviews. I understand there are many reasons why authors seek only positive reviews. For example, some of the book subscription services mentioned earlier in this book only promote books with a certain star rating. BookBub, for example, actually evaluates your book by looking at the number of reviews and ratings it has to determine whether it will be a featured book. Others insist on at least an average 4-star rating. So how can you be promoted on these sites if you don't have enough positive reviews? The average star rating on Amazon.com is over 4 stars, so by seeking out readers in your book genre and asking for honest reviews, you should get where you want to be. The benefits of honest reviews simply outweigh those of just positive reviews.

To prove my point further, let's examine why authors want just positive 5-star reviews. I believe this is either because they are so emotionally attached to their book (yes, it's almost like their "baby") that they find it hard to tolerate any negative comments, or, more likely, they think having only positive reviews is the best thing to influence potential buyers on Amazon.

This might surprise a good number of you, but no, this perception is wrong.

A number of studies on the buying behavior of online purchasers, including on Amazon, conclude that what the buyer is looking for is authenticity. The studies have concluded that the best-selling books tend to have a graphical "J-shape" to their reviews. Cornell researchers, for example, made a study of New York Times best-selling books and concluded that many successful books had a distribution of about 9% 1-star reviews, 5% 2-star reviews, 9% 3-star reviews, 18% 4-star reviews, and 59% 5-star reviews.

In other words, mostly 4- or 5-star reviews, but also some 1-star reviews, and a few in between. Many buyers will not only look at the most positive reviews but also the negative ones. Don't you do this, too?

Interestingly, this "J-shaped" revelation has led to further research on the matter. For instance, Nan Hu and Paul Pavlou's paper, "Overcoming the J-shaped distribution of product reviews", explains that the J-shape pattern found on most book reviews is down to the purchasing bias of the buyers. People simply buy books they think they will like. Whereas the proportion of the market that would most likely not like the book would not buy the book in the first place. So, book buyers on Amazon who post reviews are more likely to give a positive review than a negative one.

So, again, this emphasizes the importance of finding book reviewers as part of your marketing plan. Not only are they the most likely to post reviews on Amazon, but they are also the most likely to post positive reviews. Does that make them honest reviews? Absolutely. They are simply reflecting the fact that they represent your target audience, the type of people who are likely to buy your book.

Another reason for seeking reviews is provided in another study carried out by Wendy Moe and Michael Trusov, in their paper "Measuring the value of social dynamics in online product ratings forums". In it, they conclude that "book reviews not only reflect the readers' opinion of your book, but also affect the ratings of later reviews as well."

So, here we have the "follow the herd" principle again. If many reviewers indicate they like your book, or comment on a particular aspect of your book, then this will be picked up by other reviewers, too. For example, if the first reviewers comment on your book having a lot of violence and therefore best for mature readers, many other reviewers will post similar comments. Similarly, if they think the main protagonist in your novel is a gorgeous hunk, others will make similar remarks.

What can I do about negative reviews - how can I get them removed?

For the reasons I have already covered with regard to seeking out the best ways to get positive reviews, I believe buyers are looking for authenticity, so having a few negative reviews can be a good thing. What you should be asking yourself is, do the reviews of my book on Amazon look genuine and have the "J-shaped" pattern so often seen on best-selling books? If the majority of your reviews are positive and you have a few negative ones, then this should be seen as a good thing.

If, however, you have a lot of negative reviews in proportion to your positive ones, then you do have cause for concern. In these cases, examine why you are getting such negativity. Is it because the book is considered by the readers to be poorly edited with lots of grammatical and spelling mistakes? Or are you a victim of a troll attack where people are deliberately writing crass and negative comments with little sign of having actually read the book? Or is it that you are simply attracting the wrong type of audience, perhaps as an after-math of offering your book for free for a promotion you ran?

These are things that can be remedied with a little know how, so if you fall victim to such negativity, do contact me for ways to help you out. There are even some "black hat" methods to get bad reviews totally removed, but as with all "black hat" ideas, some consideration needs to be made before deciding to use them. Other methods involve making the bad review disappear into the background so it is not noticed, rather than having it totally removed. By asking people you know to vote up the reviews you like you can take better control of the reviews displayed on the first page of your book. Is this market manipulation? Maybe. But it's no different from publishers deciding to publish only the most glowing reviews in the Editorial Review section that appears even more prominently on the Amazon book page. Does that mean that the book got no bad editorial reviews? Of course not. Publishers will only choose the most positive reviews from the press to appear on the first page on Amazon. Is this any different?

This reminds me of one of my favorite funny marketing stories. There used to be a very popular cat food commercial on TV that finished with the punch line, "9 out of 10 cat owners prefer Product X." What they don't tell you is that it took a long time to find those 9 owners. Welcome to the world of marketing, where it's all about how you present the product.

More ingenious is the method of voting up a 1- or 2-star review that actually does not read too badly. A one-star review that draws several helpful votes and which shows that they actually thought the book was well-written but that it just wasn't their type of book will hardly discourage readers from trying out your book, and may even encourage them to buy it. In such cases, the potential buyer understands that the error is not in your book, but in the selection made by the reviewer.

Do reviews increase my Amazon Sales Ranking?

The answer depends on how you are getting the reviews. Many reviews will be posted by people who purchased your book, so their review will have the Amazon "verified purchase" badge displayed next to their review. In this case, they have purchased your book so, yes, it will increase your Amazon Sales Ranking. The value of an

Amazon "verified purchase" is also confirmed by Amazon itself. On their website they clearly state:

"The Amazon verified review label offers one more way to help gauge the quality and relevance of a product review."

You can't really be much clearer than that.

If, on the other hand, you get reviews without a verified purchase, then it has no impact on the Amazon Sales Ranking. This includes people who use Kindle Unlimited to select a book and read it. In the eyes of Amazon, customers who use Kindle Unlimited are not buying a book, but merely borrowing it until they return it in exchange for another book.

In what other ways do reviews benefit my book?

A recent change in the Amazon algorithm has made getting book reviews even more important than before. Basically, the new change gives preference to authors getting more, or rather newer, "verified purchase" reviews for their book on the Amazon store, and in getting more helpful votes.

How does this new change affect authors' books?

Firstly, your star rating used to be affected only by the star rating provided by the people writing the reviews. So, previously, Amazon would just add up all the ratings for your reviews and display the average star rating score. No more.

Today, your star rating is also affected by the number of:

- Verified purchase reviews
- Helpful votes your book reviews get
- Most recent reviews

This is a potential game-changer. This means that authors need to also seek:

- A regular stream of new reviews
- More helpful votes for the reviews that exist

While these new changes are being discussed in many forums, the implications of this are becoming quite clear. In effect, it means that if your book has not received a new review in quite a long while, it will be at a disadvantage against others that have. If your book reviews do not gather many helpful votes, it could again potentially be at a disadvantage.

In wrapping up this chapter, I hope it's clear to the reader that reviews are very important. Amazon says so, and market research says so. Equally important is to focus on finding reviewers. Data mining tools and book subscription services are a key way to find these reviewers. Sort this out, and you are well on your way to finding a good number of reviews for your book.

CHAPTER 18

THE ULTIMATE GOAL - GETTING ON THE AMAZON RADAR

WHETHER WE LIKE it or not, self-publishing authors are at a big disadvantage against traditionally published authors.

Let's discuss the first obvious disadvantage.

Unlike traditionally published authors, self-published authors have practically no presence in actual bookshops. Print distribution and lack of shelf space in bookshops and other stores is literally stacked against the self-published author. While indie authors continue to hit the Best Seller lists, their presence in bookstores remains negligible, if not non-existent. This is a shame because it is clear that indie authors can write books as well as any traditional author who has the backing of a big publishing house.

Even more of a shame is that indie authors are deprived of the sheer pleasure of seeing their books physically in a bookstore. This is important for sales, too, because while digital sales have reached the millions, most readers still prefer the printed book. Indie authors should be able to attract the types of readers who walk into book-stores – and yet they can't. However great and successful their book might be, they don't control the print distribution to stores.

The good news is that some small bookstores are beginning to include indie books, but they remain incredibly small in number, and the chances of getting in these stores remain very small. The issue is one of discoverability. Most booksellers and libraries alike order their titles through online catalogues that don't include self-published books. So, if an indie author's book can't be found in the catalogues— where every traditional publisher from Abrams to Simon & Schuster list their titles—then there is no chance at all.

The second major challenge or barrier facing indie authors is the lack of traditional media coverage. Despite self-publishing authors making the big-time Best Seller lists both on Amazon and The New York Times, and having lots of social media support, recognition from the traditional literary community is practically non-existent. Few, if any, top book reviewers published in the traditional newspapers and magazines will cover indie titles. They just don't know, or want to know, about self-published books, however good some of them might be.

In part, this is due to the great mass of self-published books being published – there are simply too many of them to cover, and many of them (let's face it) are well below par. There are some very reputable and established outlets like Kirkus and Self-Publishing Review that will cover indie authors, but these are the few among the many. As before, media coverage is reserved for the traditional publishing deals.

The best option for self-published authors is to sell within the Amazon universe.

Become successful within Amazon, and you will achieve the next best thing to having your book in multiple bookstores and covered in the press. In some ways, this is the new age of publishing. Online visibility is becoming as important as visibility in the brick-and-mortar stores, which remain the terrain of the big publishing houses. If you can't beat the big publishers in the bookstores, then beat them in the new and engaging world of the online store - and where better to do this than on Amazon.com, the biggest online bookstore in the world?

Consider the Amazon store as your new arena now. Just like the gladiators of the Roman era, you must learn to fight, knowing what it takes to not only survive, but to thrive in this new digital world.

Become visible and sell well in the Amazon store – this should be your main ambition now. Perhaps one day you might prefer for your books to be published by a traditional publisher and sold in the big bookstores. Or perhaps you'd like to become a successful hybrid author with your eBooks published independently by yourself, and your printed books to be published and promoted by a large publisher.

All good and well, but your focus for now should be on Amazon.com. Follow the methods I have described in this book and you will become more visible within the Amazon universe. Find enough new readers and sales, and Amazon itself will become your sales champion, selling your books for you. It will do this by recommending your book in the many ways we have already covered in this book.

The way Amazon promotes books is changing rapidly, but the fundamentals are all laid out in this book. Amazon will continue to introduce new ways to help promote and sell your book. For example, Amazon Ads were introduced not so long ago, and are now becoming very popular, so newer ways of promoting your book are bound to come up.

This will certainly change further in the years to come, but if there is one thing I am sure of, it's that Amazon will remain on the cutting edge of the best ways to sell books online.

If any of you have seen the film "Minority Report" starring Tom Cruise, you might recall advertising billboards which can recognize passers-by, target them with customized adverts, and even use their names. We are not there yet. But with Amazon, we are one step closer to this future world of advertising. And it's one all authors should want to be part of.

CHAPTER 19

SUMMARY AND NEXT ACTIONS TO TAKE

IN THE EARLY part of this book, I revealed "The Good, The Bad, and The Ugly" side of eBook marketing. I highlighted many of the mistakes authors make in promoting their books. More importantly, I showed you the "good" way to market your book, encouraging you to use book subscription services.

We then looked at the eBook Marketing Magic Quadrant, which helps measure the effectiveness of a book marketing campaign, or any efforts you might want to consider in promoting your book. It introduced the idea of looking for vendors that deliver you the "best revenue" opportunity and finding the "most engaged readers" for your book.

Next, we examined the best ways to find new readers to buy your books, encouraging you to look within Amazon rather than outside it to achieve this goal.

This was followed by a quick overview of some of the more popular book promotion sites and some tips on how to ensure they accept your book.

We then focused on the importance of book reviews and some of the best ways to get them, with the principle message that you should stop seeking reviews and concentrate on finding reviewers.

Finally, I revealed how all these methods can get you detected on the Amazon radar, so that they will help you sell your book using the Amazon sales machine.

Given all the information, advice, and best practices I have shared with you, what then are your next steps to get started promoting your book?

What to do next:

Fundamentally, you have two main choices:

1) Do it yourself. Pick up many of the ideas and methods described in this book and execute them. I have shown you how you can get your book on the Amazon Best Seller lists, the Hot New Releases, and "Customers who bought this item also bought" sections of Amazon. Even getting onto Amazon's Popularity Lists can be achieved, now that you understand how it works and what it takes to get there.

All of the methods I have covered to get you there will take you some time, some careful diligence, and plenty of effort, but it is achievable. I am confident they will work for you as they have done for the hundreds of authors I have helped to achieve the same goals.

If you take this route, I encourage you to share your experiences along the way and the results you achieved. Did your book get on the Best Seller lists using the suggestions I gave you? Did you find a better category for your book? Did getting lots of reviews for your book help your sales?

2) The other main choice is to use book promotion sites (or book subscription services) from the most popular ones I have listed for you, and let them do the promotion work for you. Whether it's your

desire to get thousands of free downloads of your book into the hands of prospective buyers, or to get your book into the Amazon Best Seller list, leveraging the network of readers provided by these services can save you a lot of time and effort. Sure, you have to pay for these services, but the benefits are very clear, giving you the time and focus you need to do what you probably like to do most: write books. And remember, some of these providers even guarantee results.

I hope you have enjoyed this book and that it has provided you with ideas and even the inspiration to try out new things to promote your book.

All honest opinions about what you think of this book are welcome, and I encourage you to write a review on Amazon. If you do, send me an email. In return, I will send you a personal thanks and a copy of my "Unofficial Authors' Guide to Promoting Your Book on Amazon - The Top 5 Cheat Sheet".

I look forward to hearing from you.

CHAPTER 20

HOW TO CONTACT ME

WHETHER IT'S to discuss some of the ideas shared in this book, or to ask me to help market your book, this is the best way to contact me:

Email:
richard@kbookpromotions.com
Website:
www.kbookpromotions.com
LinkedIn:
www.linkedin.com/in/richardmccartney1

SPECIAL OFFER

Why not give kbookpromotions.com a try? Find out what it takes to make your book a Best Seller on Amazon, or to get feedback from the news readers who select your book.

What other authors have to say about the service:

"I'm speechless. Truly. Champagne on me. Seeing my book at #1 in the Best Seller lists really made me smile. I'm still rather awestruck right now over all of it. My wildest dreams I really wasn't believing it could be done. I cannot thank you enough for everything!!
Sherry Rentschler, author of Time and Blood

"Great job. You were spot on with your promise. Thanks for being so reliable in an age of hype. Will look to you in future for ideas to gain further impetus."
Doug Pope, author of Inherit the Wind.

"Oh my gosh !!!! "I'm so thrilled with the results of the promotion you ran for me! THANK YOU FROM THE BOTTOM OF MY HEART! I'm very grateful. To finally be heard after being silent for so long. There are no words. "
Jena Parks, author of The Fear of the Blow

Authors reading this book and who would like to try out kbookpromotions for the first time can ask for a $40 discount.

$40 for having finished reading a book! Now there's a good deal.

For your free $40 coupon, just send an email to the following address:

richard@kbookpromotions.com

Thanking you - Richard

ABOUT THE AUTHOR

Richard McCartney has been helping authors promote their books for several years now. Some describe him as that British guy who is always helping authors out with new ideas to promote their books.

He lives in The Netherlands with his wife and three daughters, and his only male companion is his Jack Russell who he sits in front of the TV screen to keep him company while watching football (since nobody else in the house is interested).

Beyond that he will rarely be drawn. Who reads these biographies, anyway? Readers just want to get on with reading the book, and not wade through pages about an author trying to convince others that he is cool and sophisticated, or highly skilled at something.

Yet if you really must know, he is the founder of kbookpromotions, listed as one of the Best Book Promotions sites of 2018 and 2019 by Paid Author. He is also author of books such as:

- The Unofficial Authors Guide To Selling Your Book On Amazon
- Self-Publishing: The Secret Guide To Becoming A Best Seller
- Self-Publishing Disruption: Marketing tips that work so well it Feels like Cheating.

In his search for a quiet life, he avoided all the really interesting jobs many authors add to make their biographies look interesting. And yes, it's true, Jack Russells don't like watching football either - so that's why he takes him high-cliff diving too. He loves it!

This book is going to show you the top 5 secrets to selling your book on Amazon.

These are rock solid proven tips that are sure to make your book more visible on the only online store that counts – Amazon.

Self-Publishing Disruption: marketing tips that work so well it feels like cheating.

Discover how to:

- get to page 1 of Amazon's search results
- find the best book promotion sites
- discover new readers in your genre?

The Unofficial Authors Guide To Selling Your Book On Amazon